AF486356

THE STICKY NOTE PLOT

PRAISE FOR THE STICKY NOTE PLOT

A brilliant, accessible resource for every writer. A must-read."

A.S. KING, TWO-TIME MICHAEL L.
AWARD RECIPIENT

"Ever since learning David Gill's Sticky Note Plotting in 2015, I have used it for every novel I've written (& sold)! This visual method works perfectly for me!"

—DEBBI MICHIKO FLORENCE, AUTHOR
OF THE JASMINE TOGUCHI SERIES

THE STICKY NOTE PLOT

A STEP-BY-STEP GUIDE TO NOVELS THAT SELL

DAVID MACINNIS GILL

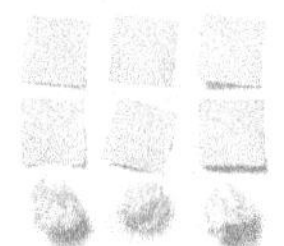

CONTENTS

Published by Thunderchikin Ink.

Designed by Martha Brockenbrough

Copyright 2024 by David Macinnis Gill. All rights reserved under International and Pan-American Copyright Conventions. Printed in the United States of America. No part of this book may be used or reproduced in any manner without written permission of the author, except in the case of brief quotations published in the context of critical articles or reviews.

By payment of fees, the reader has been granted the nonexclusive, nontransferable right to read the text of this book. No part of this text may be reproduced, transmitted, decompiled, reverse-engineered, used to train AI, or stored in any form or by any means, electronic or mechanical, without the express written permission of the publisher.

The Sticky Note Plot, Sticky Note Wall, The Sticky Note Plot Method, Spreadsheet of Doom, and associated phrases and descriptions of processes are the copyrighted intellectual property of David Macinnis Gill.

 Created with Vellum

PART 1

THE
STICKY NOTE PLOT
PROCESS

CHAPTER 1
A WORD ABOUT THE THREE-ACT STRUCTURE

BEFORE WE GET INTO THE NITTY-GRITTY of the Sticky Note Plot process, we need to talk about story structure. A long time ago, circa 335 BC, Aristotle published a treatise called *Poetics*, which was an examination of literary theory. Some people know it as the seminal work of Western theatre, but I think of it as the first-ever master's thesis. Even in the early part of our development with drama, writers were analyzing the work that they were doing at the time. And they were drawing conclusions.

In *Poetics*, Aristotle focused on drama as one of the three literary forms (the other two being lyric poetry and epic). For examples of his theories, he used the theatre that was so culturally important in Greece at the time. The structure of novels is very similar to the structure of drama, and we're still using his ideas to define stories today.

Aristotle noticed that successful plays all had similar plot architecture. The plots had the same segments or "acts"—a beginning, a middle, and an end. It may seem obvious and simplistic to say that, but you might be surprised at how many novels (usually unsuccessful ones) lack one of the three acts. My early novels sure did. Of course, Aristotle, being Greek, used Greek words to name the acts. He used the terms prolog, episode, and exodus which meant beginning, middle, and end. Drama and fiction have three acts. However, those acts are subdivided, and that's the way it's been since 335 B.C.

No matter what forms drama has taken since Aristotle's time—different characters, different settings, different playwrights, different genres—the same basic three acts, the beginning, the middle, and the end, have remained. That makes sense, doesn't it? Yet, for something that seems so obvious, dramatic structure can be so elusive, it becomes almost ethereal. It's really difficult to pin down. It certainly was for me, and the best way I found to pin it down was to stick it to a wall.

A couple of caveats before we get into the weeds of the three-act structure: We writers often look for craft tips to help us understand our work and process. We are always looking to get better, to get faster, to be more successful, and there are thousands of opinions about how to accomplish writing goals. Sometimes, those opinions get stated as hard and fast, unbreakable rules. It's easier to get mired in the didacticism of The Things We Must Do.

The fact is, there are no must dos in writing fiction. Writers can do anything we want to do. Because it's our own world. It lives in our brain. Our fingers are on the keyboard and as we type, as we dictate, as we move a pen or pencil to move ink or graphite across a sheet of paper, we make all the decisions. Bwahaha! What awesome power. What awesome responsibility. What a beautiful way to make ourselves crazy, because along with the ability to decide how a story can go comes the self-doubt about which way the story should go. When that self-doubt sinks in, we can make our lives harder than necessary. Writing is difficult enough. So when I tell you about story structure and things you can do within it, I'm not talking about rules you must follow. I'm talking about techniques that can make your writing life easier. Think can, not must. Can is infinite story possibilities. Must is a creative dead end.

Think yes, not no.

The word about the three-act structure is "yes."

Yes, it exists. Yes, it's found in almost every story. Yes, it's possible to write a novel that doesn't conform to it. Yes, doing so makes the job that much harder. But it's worth it.

A BRIEF OVERVIEW OF THE MODERN THREE-ACT PLOT STRUCTURE

David Bowie's "Modern Love" is playing in my head (just ignore the humming). Bowie was always pushing boundaries, expanding the concept of what music and artistry could be, but his music fundamentals were always evident. The concept of the modern three-act structure has evolved, but its fundamentals remain the same. Once upon a time (like before the 1990s), the length of each of the three acts was roughly the same, which was about one-third of a novel, or with Hollywood cinema, about one-third of a movie. Act 1 would be the setup, Act 2 would be the bulk of the action, and Act 3 would be the ending.

The 1985 film *Witness*, for example, is almost exactly one-third for each section. In the first act, Rachel and her young son Samuel visit Baltimore, where Samuel witnesses a murder. In the second act, John Book goes on the run with Rachel and Samuel, back to their Pennsylvania Amish community so that Book can protect Samuel until the trial. In the last act, the bad guys (trying to avoid spoilers in case you want to watch it) arrive and try to take out the witness.

The story structure of *Witness* is an almost perfect balance, but few modern readers would have the patience for a story that takes so long to develop. We want the action to begin more quickly. We want more stuff to happen in the middle. We want endings to be more final. In response to this change of taste (I won't call it a lack of patience), writers have shortened Acts 1 and 3, and we have expanded Act 2 so that it takes up a full one-half of the novel, not just one-third of it.

Having a longer Act 2 means the middle is much longer, which leaves room for more complications and more suspense. But a longer Act 2 makes it easier for the middle to turn into a muddle, and muddles make our writing lives harder. Since my goal is to make your writing life easier, I'm going to start off by explaining what each Act of a novel does, and I'm going to show you how to use story structure to save time and make the story loud (remember that my first few novels were rejected for being "too quiet"?). This is important information, and we will be coming to it again later when we get micro with the Sticky Note Plot process and then again when we discuss Key Scenes.

ACT 1: KEY SCENES IN ACTION

Act 1 is the beginning of the story. It has specific, essential story elements that need to be included, starting with the setting. Setting is the time, place, and culture of the story, often called **"The World As It Is."** This term and many of the terms I use to describe the important scenes are adapted by Joseph Campbell's *The Hero with a Thousand Faces*. Published in 1949, the book draws inspiration from Carl Jung's psychoanalytical theories to assemble a unified theory of narrative, which Campbell termed the monomyth. Campbell based his work on previous scholars such as Edward Tylor and Otto Rank. Many know Campbell's theory as the Hero's Journey, which is a circular pattern that includes terms that match somewhat the Key Scenes that I use for the Sticky Note Plot. While Campbell was only describing narratives as he observed them, writers soon began using the monomyth pattern to plot out their stories. George Lucas famously used it to write the screenplay of Star Wars. You can use the monomyth to help craft a novel, too.

The Inciting Event is the first catalyst in the story, an event that propels changes the action of the story and pushes the characters forward. Once we have established the world, that world changes.

Think of the old Wile E. Coyote and Road Runner car toons. There is a rock poised on the side of a cliff with a small stick holding it. That is the World As It Is. The Road Runner runs by and trips a wire. This stick is released, and the ball starts rolling. That is the Inciting Event.

It can be easy to write Act 1 because it's home to the Inciting Event, and that's where the fun is. Inciting Events are the genesis of the story, the premise, the creation engine that gets the juices flowing. It's usually the first thing that happens after the world is established. Once the Coyote's rock ball starts rolling, it cannot be stopped, and that is the same momentum you need from your own Inciting Event. Suggestion: Keep the Inciting Event scene short. Don't spread it out. Write only as much as you need to establish what that event is, the one moment at the beginning of the novel that starts the ball rolling and nothing can stop it.

After the Inciting Event in Act 1, there's a Call to Action. In the Call to Action, the hero is given a task. In Lord of the Rings, Frodo and Sam go out into the world to return the ring. In *The Hunger Games*, Katniss takes her sister's place at the Reaping. Think of the Call to Action as the moment when the character goes into motion.

Following the Call, the hero will be asked/forced/tricked/fill-in-the-blank to act or react. I call this phase the Agitation because it literally agitates the hero and forces them into action. It will be clear that the world is broken and needs to be fixed.

During or after the Agitation, a Challenge will be put forth to the hero. No matter who originates the Challenge, this scene will be about the hero accepting the responsibility of the Challenge, what ever that responsibility will be.

How does a writer agitate and then Challenge their hero? Bribery works as a motivator. Guilt does, too. So does a sense of justice, the need for revenge, or the willingness to sacrifice for others. Combining reasons makes the decision more motivating. In the Agitation and Challenge scenes, the hero may develop what novelist Martine Leavitt terms a controlling belief, which is a misunderstanding of the nature of the problem at hand and a flawed belief in how to fix it. The controlling belief often leads to a misbelief, which are false beliefs that characters hold about themselves. Since the hero is planning to act on that misbelief, you can see how events might go awry later in the story.

At this point, the hero can act in a variety of ways. They can accept the Call or reluctantly take half measures. The hero can also refuse the Call at first, and other characters may have to talk them into it. A reluctant hero is not a bad hero, and it raises conflict and stakes if the hero is not completely sold on the idea. At the end of the first act, there is a Key Scene that's in almost every novel, and that's where the hero accepts the responsibility and begins a new journey, aka The Hero's Journey. There's a reason, structurally, the journey happens here. Act 2A will be about the hero's journey. It also allows the hero to assemble a crew. Unlike the Inciting Event, which is a very specific moment in the story, the Challenge Accepted can happen throughout multiple scenes. Just make sure that the hero accepts the challenge before Act 1 is over. Act 2 can't start without it.

As with most new and exciting projects, Act 1 is the easiest to write and usually, the most fun. The shiny new idea is fresh in your mind, and story ideas are flowing. All doors are open, and all roads lead to someplace worth going. Then reality sets in, and you realize that a shiny first act does not a whole novel make, and a ton of story decisions are lurking in the shadows.

ACT 2A: WHERE THE SHADOWS RISE

Once the premise is established in Act 1, you may know how the story ends. You may even visualize the final scene. The ending may change after you create the first draft. It may remain the same. Either way, an ending gives you a target to shoot for. But how do you reach the target? How do you go from the incident event all the way to the final scene? It starts with reconceptualizing the Middle and the Midpoint. That means we no longer view Act 2A as one big chunk.

Instead, we divide it into three parts—Act 2A, the Turn, and Act 2B. Let's look at the first part, 2A.

When Act 2A starts, the character has answered the Call to Action and are beginning a new journey. The hero is now on whatever emotional or psychological or physical journey they started in Act 1. At first, they do well on the journey. They gather friends. Hijinks quickly ensue, and the stars are aligning for them and their friends. The scenes that follow these are what I call the Hero's Montage (which covers several scenes), in which the hero has a series of small victories. If they are learning to fight, the montage is made of the scenes where they go from the novice warrior to the deadliest warrior in the tribe. Think Wonder Woman here.

Or, if this is an 80s teen comedy, this is where the hero of Can't Buy Me Love, Patrick Dempsey, learns how to dress for success or Jennifer Beals' character, Alex, learns to flash-dance like a maniac. These scenes are often light and fun because the hero is succeeding, and it seems inevitable that they will be able to reach the goal quickly and successfully. The keyword here is *seems*.

Building Bridges is the part (usually a series of scenes) where the hero and their friends go from a loose group of strangers to a cohesive unit. If you apply this concept to a job or a school setting, it's where the hero forms relationships with close friends in the office or in the classroom and expands their social universe. If this is a love story, it's where they not only fall in love with that special person but also become part of their new person's life. The key element of this part is that relationships are created...so that we can destroy them later. By the end of Act 2A, it looks as if Hero & Company will easily achieve their goal.

Victory is at hand!

THE TURN: THE HINGE THAT MAKES OR BREAKS YOUR NOVEL

Yeah, no, on that victory. At the end of Act 2A, the apparent victory suddenly turns to defeat, creating a False Victory. Far from succeeding, Hero & Company are now failing, and that failure is caused by the events of the most important part of Act 2, the Turn, which is the most essential scene in the entire novel.

I didn't invent the term the Turn. I didn't invent the term Midpoint, either, but I conceptualize it a little bit differently than some of the other plot gurus out there, and later in this book, I will show you how I use it in my own work and how you can find it in other authors' work, as well. The best way that I can describe how I conceptualize the Turn is this:

Envision a makeup compact.

It is a single object with two parts held together by a hinge in the middle. There is a mirror on each side of the compact, then when you close the compact, it looks like a single object. When you open the compact, it becomes obvious that it is two parts held together by that hinge. The hinge is the Turn.

The Turn is where everything goes wrong. That's where this stuff hits the fan. Everything that the hero got right in the beginning? They will screw it up in Act 2B (more on Act 2B below). Remember the victory that Hero & Company almost reached? It doesn't happen, and in fact, they face defeat. By the end of Act 2, the hero is humbled and almost destroyed. The destruction is caused by the Turn.

As I mentioned before, the middle of a novel is commonly called the Midpoint. That's a misnomer. It makes it sound like you've gotten halfway across the country on a coast-to-coast trip, one that you could still turn back from. The middle of the story needs to be more than just a halfway point. It needs to be an event that turns the story on its ear, a significant, irreversible change that the hero (and the reader) cannot return from. At the Turn, the story changes fundamentally. One or more characters are so altered, they are forever changed, and that change catapults the hero and other characters through the rest of the story.

A great Turn fixes the muddle of the middle because it makes Act 2B, which will be the antithesis of Act 2A, absolutely imperative. What makes a great Turn? One that changes the story physically, emotionally, or catastrophically. It causes great damage to the hero and to the people that the hero cares most about.

Physical Turns: If you cut off the character's hand, it can't grow back (depending on the genre) so they are changed permanently. In The Game of Thrones, Jaime Lannister gets his right hand lopped off. The greatest swordsman in Westeros, he must now fight left-handed, and he is no Inigo Montoya. Has he changed? Yes. Has he changed for the better? One could argue that lopping off Jamie's hand made him a better person (I'm not sure that was true, because in the end, he made the same bad decisions), but it made him a much worse swordsman. The plot, that change matters, and you can make it matter more.

Emotional Turns: In this Turn, the hero gets their heart broken. It can be a breakup, or a bitter defeat, or the loss of a loved one. The most difficult Emotional Turn to pull off is a secret revealed. That's where a character finds out something about another character (or about themselves) that fundamentally changes how they see the other character and themselves. If the reader finds out the secret at the same time as the hero, it changes the reader's perception of that character. Double whammy!

Catastrophic Turns: If you've seen a disaster movie from the 70s, catastrophe was evidently all studios had. They did cruise ship movies. They did airplanes. They did earthquakes, tsunamis, and volcanoes. Why? Maybe because it was easy. Any "Act of God" has the ability to alter the setting. Disaster is a simple way to create a Turn. If an author chooses a high-rise building as a setting, knocking down the building fundamentally changes the story. It worked well until audiences grew tired of catastrophes, then the spoofs like Airplane! came out. While the trope had legs, the disasters are just shortcuts if they don't tie into the arcs of the characters themselves. Combo Turns: Want a truly powerful Turn? Combine all three—physical, emotional, and catastrophic—into one single Turn. It's very effective but very difficult to pull off because you have to align all of the actions into what is usually a single event. That takes lots of planning, and it's where using sticky notes to plot helps you early on in the process.

Regardless of planning, the Turn often does not reveal itself easily. That's usually because you don't know your desire line well enough yet. Try examining the cast of characters. Maybe do side writing or character work to understand why the Turn would mean so much to them. Think about the assumptions you've made about the characters. Dig more deeply into them. Find their emotional core. Find things they care most about. Then at the Turn, take all that important stuff away.

Every single bit.

As one of my clients said, "After you see the Turn, you won't be able to unsee it." Instead of having this amorphous blob of a story that wanders everywhere, you will have a middle that becomes more than a series of rest stops on a cross-country tour. The plot will have a new direction, which some of my students have termed, "The Beginning of the End." No matter what kind of Turn you come up with, it has to be tied directly to the hero and what they want—their desires. So don't force it: The Turn is there to help you.

ACT 2B: WHERE THE SHADOWS FALL, AKA THE SKINNIEST ACT

If there is a place where you're going to struggle during the first draft, it is in writing Act 2B. This will probably be the thinnest act when you create your own Sticky Note Plot (we'll get there soon), and Act 2B will have the fewest scenes in the story beat sheet (more on beat sheets in a later chapter). Why? Because that part of the story hasn't bloomed in your brain yet and because you are concentrating on the wrong character, the hero. The hero has been driving the story up to this point, but it's time for them to take a backseat. In Act 2B, other characters will rise up to fill out the story, allowing you ways to flesh out Act 2B more completely.

Traditionally, when talking about a novel, we have framed the conversation around the main plot and subplots. Let's set that definition aside. Instead, let's think about novel plots in terms of A-story and B-story. The A-story is the hero's plot. Every other plot is a B-Story. There are no subplots, and there are no C-stories.

The most obvious B-Story is the antagonist's plot, which I call the Villain's Montage. Remember in Act 2A, the hero had their montage where everything went great? Now the villain will have their own montage, in which everything goes great...for the villain. Behind the scenes for the whole book, the villain has been working on their plan, and here's where it finally comes into view. In the first half of the novel, the hero drives the action of the novel. Now it is the antagonist's turn to drive the action, which leads to a phase I call Burning Bridges. Remember Building Bridges from Act 2A? Burning Bridges is the opposite, the antithesis, of those scenes in Act 2A, where the relationships the hero built with secondary characters now fall apart. Speaking of secondary characters, Act 2B is the place for those characters to have their moment in the sun. Like the protagonist, a well-rounded secondary character has their own set of goals and a desire line.

The common definition of desire line is "an unplanned route or path (such as one worn into a grassy surface by repeated foot traffic) that is used by pedestrians in preference to or in the absence of a designated alternative." For fiction writers, I define a desire line as "the interconnected route, direct or indirect, that a character takes while pursuing their ultimate goal." In Act 2B, the secondary characters get the chance to flaunt their desire lines. Why not? The hero is busy getting whacked by the villain's plan. A cool thing about secondary characters' goals is that their desire line can weave into the hero's desire line, run parallel to it, or run in contrast to it. So in

Act 2B, their goals can entangle themselves with the hero, give support to the hero, or oppose the hero.

This is the scene where secondary characters' desire lines come into focus. It is also the most difficult sequence for me to describe. Unlike Acts 1 and 2A, the B-Story has to arise from the events you created in the first half of the novel. The events of Acts 1 and 2A will decide the events and the order of events in Act 2B, so there is no specific way that a B-Story comes to focus on this section. In short, the other characters need to step up, and the hero needs to step back. When this happens, Act 2B reaches its potential and leads directly to the final scene, the hero's False Defeat, where they look to be utterly defeated. This is the antithesis of the scene that closed Act 2A, the False Victory.

ACT 3: THE END

We have reached the beginning of the ending. Like the other Act 1, Act 3 has specific elements. These elements may vary based on genre expectations and length. Typically, the elements are a promise of self-evaluation by the hero, a final battle with the villain that completes the challenge the hero accepted in Act 1, and a return to equilibrium so that The World As It Is becomes The World As It Will Be.

During the Sticky Note Plot process, Act 3 might be easy to visualize. You can probably see a long scene of reflection, a battle with the villain, or an epilogue where our hero is reunited with their loved ones. As you write a draft, though, the events you saw so clearly may have to change completely. That's because Act 3, the ending, is mostly determined by the character development in the aftermath of the Turn than by what happened in earlier Acts.

Character development reaches its peak at the beginning of Act 3. At the end of Act 2B, our hero faced a False Defeat. They are now experiencing the Dark Night of the Soul—that long scene of self-reflection they are at their lowest possible point. Everything they worked for is lost. They have no marbles left in the game. Or so it seems. There is something left in the tank—an inkling of hope—that sparks a soul-searching epiphany.

The hero forms a New Plan of Action, maybe because of a rescue or maybe calls up new strength forged in defeat and sets out to defeat the villain once and for all.

However, the final battle ends, be it an epic battle or low-key confrontation, and the hero is victorious. This leads us to the final part of Act 3, The World As It Will Be. These last scenes of the novel put a bow on the story, show that the hero has survived, and let the reader know that the world that went off kilter at the start of Act 1 has returned to equilibrium. In my novel *Uncanny*, the World As It Is scene is presented as an epilogue set in the near future of the novel's timeline. It shows the hero, Willow Jane, even though she has faced a loss, has survived and will carry on.

Take a minute and think about most of the novel endings that you've found unsatisfying. Chances are, they left the reader hanging by not showing that equilibrium has been restored. Readers need some sort of resolution, even if the ending is meant to be open-ended. Remember: Plot is the series of actions a character does because of what those actions mean to them. The ending has to mean something, too.

Let me anticipate a question that may be forming in your mind: You may be wondering, must I have a Turn? Or a villain? Or a character desire line?

The answer is no.

Did that surprise you? Despite what you may have read elsewhere, there are no musts in novel writing. You don't have to include a specific plot element or character. You're the writer. The story lives in your mind. It appears to the world through your fingers on the keyboard. You don't have to have a three-act structure. You don't have to have an Inciting Event and a Call to Action. Or follow the steps of the Hero's Journey. Or have a villain. Or follow any of the suggestions I've made. Many successful novels have been created without these elements.

Then why follow the Sticky Note Plotting process?

Because your writing process will be easier if you do, especially if you've never finished a first draft. Writing a novel is already a difficult and time-consuming undertaking. Why start off making the process harder than it has to be?

Let's start making it easier.

21

ACTIVITIES:
DIGGING DEEPER

THE THREE-ACT STRUCTURE IS UBIQUITOUS in Western storytelling, whether it's fiction, film, or graphic novels. For some novelists, though, the structure can be difficult to internalize. For them, the structure feels less like it's guiding their planning and more like it's forcing them to fit their stories into a box. Take a minute to think about these questions:

- Is the Three-act structure intuitive to you? Or do you struggle to wrap your brain around it? Does the concept of structure feel like it constrains your ideas? Or does it give you a scaffolding to support your imagination?
- If the Three-act structure isn't feeling right, can you think of other ways that you could tell a story? Are there other patterns that you could use? Take a look at other forms of storytelling. There may be a less common way to tell a story.
- Assuming you find another type of story structure, how can you apply the Sticky Note Plot process to that

structure? You can find more details about the Sticky Note Plot process in Chapter Two.

- If you can't find another structure or if you'd really like to understand the intricacies of the Three-act structure, you can try to immerse yourself in story. When I was in this same situation, I watched countless films on Netflix. Except that I set the viewing speed to 2x and watched with the sound off. This helped me recognize the ways that screenwriters and directors used the same patterns to visually convey important action in Key Scenes. Try it and see if it works for you.

EXERCISE 1

Pick up your favorite novel. Open the book to the middle, then go five pages back. Read the next ten pages or so. Is there a midpoint Turn? What kind is it? What happens to the hero? Is their misbelief exposed? How does the change affect the rest of the novel?

EXERCISE 2

Think about the premise of a current work in progress. Is the premise a cool idea? A unique twist on an old trope? A dilemma for the hero? Most importantly, is it about a main character in the novel? If it is, how can you make the premise more personal for the character? If it's not about a character but about the plot, how can you tweak the premise so that its outcomes affect the hero or another main character? How does the premise affect the hero's beliefs and misbeliefs?

EXERCISE 3

In this chapter, I described the Turn as the hinge on a compact (or a clamshell). Draw a picture of the compact. Label the left side "2A" and the right side "2B." List a few positive characteristics of the hero on the left. On the right, list the negative opposite of those characteristics. What could happen at the Turn that would make the hero change characteristics from positive to negative?

STICKY NOTE CHECKLIST: WHY USE STRUCTURE?

- To give you a clothesline to hang your story laundry.
- To tap into the collective unconsciousness of reader expectations.
- To avoid the twin curse of "too quiet" and "too episodic."
- To prevent you from ever having to ask the question, "okay, what the &%#$ happens now?" when you write yourself off the cliff at page one hundred.
- To preempt the dreaded "???" that beta readers scribble all over the margins when they can't figure out why in the world the characters would ever do such a thing.
- To ditch that panicked feeling when the little voice inside you says, "It's okay, no one will notice that the book abruptly ends in the last ten pages."
- To sell the manuscript to a publisher who just can't put it down.

CHAPTER 2
THE STICKY NOTE PLOT

HERE'S THE QUESTION YOU'VE BEEN WAITING FOR me to answer: What is the Sticky Note Plot? The answer is simple, and that's the magic of this plotting system—it's simple. Sticky Note Plot is a story creation process model that I've developed over time. It's for writers who want to plot out a novel as efficiently as possible and to brainstorm as easily as possible, but still want to capture that brainstorming and to put it in some kind of order.

HOW THE STICKY NOTE PLOTTING PROCESS WORKS

To do a Sticky Note Plot, you need sticky notes. They need to be at least four different (five is even better) colors, and you need something to write with. I prefer Sharpies so I can read the notes across the room. Oh yeah, you also need a wall. Preferably a blank wall with lots of room that's not prone to moisture. Sticky notes will drop from a moist wall like falling leaves, so consider getting the ones with a super sticky backing. Or you can do what I do, purchase one of the large sticky chart paper pads, put it on a wall, and then put the sticky notes on it. Chart paper pads tend to be expensive, so please consider them optional.

THE FIRST STEP: LABELING THE ACTS

Mark off the columns of the Three-act plot. Label the sticky notes as Act 1, Act 2A, T (for the Turn), Act 2B, and Act 3.

Tip: Once you start plotting, leave the Sticky Note Plot on the wall until it's done, no matter how long it takes. Weeks, months, even years. Its presence will remind you to keep working. It will also publicly announce that you are working on a novel and require time, think space, and an unending supply of favorite desserts and beverages (kudos if you actually get those).

Remember—and I can't emphasize this enough—you will not finish a Sticky Note Plot in one sitting. It may take days or weeks to get the plot where it needs to be. The important thing is to start the process and allow your mind the time and focus it needs to generate story ideas. Generating ideas takes time and opportunity, and it allows our subconscious to marinate the story so that we come up with something fresh and original and exciting. To summarize:

- Get the good stickies and try to find five colors.
- Cheap stickies tend to fall off walls easily, and if your dog is like mine, they will love the taste of the glue. There's nothing worse than the dog eating all your hard work.
- If you still have trouble with stickies falling, get a pack of sticky chart paper from your local favorite office supply. Good stickies will definitely stick to the chart paper.
  There are plots on my office wall that have been up for years.

TIME TO START PLOTTING: THE PROMISE OF THE PREMISE

You can start the process with a premise, a hero, an exciting event, or even an interesting setting. Whatever you prefer. For me it's almost always the premise. Sometimes, those premises just pop into my head. Sometimes, they emerge from writing exercises. Sometimes, I find them by reading articles (such as a story in science magazine about terraforming Mars via greenhouse gases that led to my novel *Black Hole Sun*). Sometimes, they're weird human-interest stories. When a premise strikes my fancy, I ask myself, does the premise have promise? Do I have any idea where the story might go? Will I love the characters enough to sustain me through multiple drafts? Can I hear a voice? Write your premise on a sticky note and put it right on the wall under Act 1. Feels good, doesn't it? Feels kind of scary, too, right? That's good. Writers need healthy doses of fear and exhilaration to keep tapping the creative well.

What else can you write on a sticky note? Anything! Literally, anything pops into your head. Setting details. Character traits. Secrets the character knows. Backstory about the world. Visuals of what certain scenes will look like. Pets. Problems. Questions. All of it. Write it down, put it on the wall! It's just a sticky note!

Now, we begin brainstorming. Sticky notes hit the wall. Cool ideas pop, and we have a ton of them, because like I said, we're just generating ideas for scenes, setting, and characters. Any and every cool idea will get us started—and so will bad ones. We're not editing or judging. Just generating sticky notes. We're seeking the imaginative spark that starts a novel, the overpowering thing that drives us to write it. Remember that drive, because we will tap into it later on to motivate us to finish our task.

The goal is to propagate a ton of stickies for the first part of the novel. Imagine that you are filling the Act 1 column with stickies. You aren't just writing down plot points. Anything relevant to the story can go on the wall scenes, settings, moments, snippets of dialogue. Write them down. Stick them up.

But why sticky notes instead of a cork board and notecards? Stickies are small, and you write big. A Sharpie writes bigger than a ballpoint pen, and it helps to write big. Because stickies are small, you can only put a little bit of information on them at once. Notecards allow you to put too much stuff on them. You can write on the front. You can write on the back. You can write small. You can write an entire scene on that note card, and if you're like me, once you've written an entire scene, you are loath to get rid of that scene, even if it doesn't work anymore.

Throwing things away is an essential part of the Sticky Note Plotting process. Also, The Sticky Note Plot is portable. You've always got some sticky notes, and all you've got to do is write one little thing on the sticky note, all right? Carry a pad of sticky notes with you. Drop a couple in the car. Put some in your bag or on the nightstand. That way, whether you're at the grocery or at the movies or waiting in the carpool line, if inspiration strikes, you'll be ready to sticky note it.

HOW IT USUALLY GOES: FIXING THE HOLES WHERE THE PLOT GETS OUT

This is how the Sticky Note Plotting process has gone for most writers I work with. As you flesh out the plot, you get lots of ideas for Act 1. A few more for Act 2A. Almost nothing for Act 2B. Finally, for Act 3, you can think of one or two scenes that you absolutely must have. There are a ton of holes in the plot after the first rush of sticky notes. That's okay. No, it's better than okay. It is preferable because filling in those holes is where the magic happens.

When I was generating stickies for my novel *Uncanny*, three scenes came to me immediately: an inciting event at a bus stop, a scary hotel scene, and a final face-off between the hero, Willow Jane, and the villain, the Shadowless. I didn't know much about the hero except that she was a hockey player, and I knew nothing about the villain except that she carried wicked long shears. But I saw that fight in my mind's eye. The details of the fight went on the board, and that scene went into the book.

Creating the plot structure is a process—you won't sit down in five minutes and create a whole novel. At first, your plots will look unbalanced. It takes time and thought to generate scenes that flow organically from Act 1. So if you see an unbalanced pattern on your Sticky Note Wall, don't be discouraged. Things take time.

How long? It depends on you and the story. But you won't do it in five minutes. Or five hours, Or five days. Well, maybe in five days if the muse is really singing. Carry a Sharpie and stack of stickies with you. Let the ideas percolate, generate, marinate. Keep scribbling till you have 60-80 notes on the wall. If you get stuck, then turn your attention to the two most important characters: protagonists and antagonists.

CHARACTER ARCS: PROTAGONISTS AND ANTAGONISTS

Everyone loves a hero. We root for them. We cheer for them. We fall in love with them. We hurt for them. But they don't exist in a vacuum. They need someone to fight. The most common question I get asked when I lead workshops is: does my story have to have a villain? The answer is easy. No, you don't have to have a villain. But life is easier if you do.

It is possible to write a story without an antagonist at all. Those stories do exist. It's just easier to have a human villain who can actively oppose the hero. To borrow a cliché, steel needs a hammer to temper it, to give it strength. For the protagonist to develop and grow throughout the story, to become a true hero, they have to strive against something that is almost as powerful as they are.

Everyone hates a villain, but a great villain can make any story better. Think about Darth Vader. He was the villain of the first Star Wars Trilogy, yet he was by far the most compelling character for many fans. Vader was powerful, he was strong, he was pursuing a clear goal, and he had a deep yearning that could not be satisfied. The fact that he was evil had nothing to do with his success. Like many great villains, Vader truly believed that he was doing the right thing, even though his methods left a lot to be desired. That's the key to any great villain. They have their own story arc, which just so happens to run contrary to the hero's goals, development, and yearning. It is that contrast that creates the most conflict, the higher stakes, and the deepest character development. So even if you think you don't need an antagonist, give it a go, and try to make the best one you can.

THE SETTING: THE HIDDEN CHARACTER

In simplest terms, setting is the time and place of the story. A great setting is more than a description of the atmosphere, it is an intricate part of the story stakes, conflict among the characters, and the overall design of the novel. It adds elements like history, culture, and language, which create a fictional universe that feels authentic. It can give a unifying theme and lay the foundation for emotional resonance.

Setting also makes the novel unique. No one wants to read a story that could take place anywhere. They want to be grounded in a specific time and place, to be told the story that can only happen here and nowhere else. Some writers decide to create a generic setting, thinking that doing so lends a universal quality to the world-building. In fact, the opposite is true. Since it can happen anywhere, a generic setting happens nowhere. A universal story appeals to everyone because it's about universal themes, not because of where it is set.

Carl Hiaasen's novel *Hoot* is set in South Florida near the Everglades, a place that is overrun with tourists, retirees, sleazy politicians, and unscrupulous developers. The hero is a new kid in town, where a developer wants to bulldoze a bunch of cute burrowing owls that nest in the ground. *Hoot* could not exist anywhere else—because of those owls and because of Florida's crazy laws that let somebody bulldoze wildlife.

Louis Sachar's novel *Holes* takes place in Camp Green Lake. But Camp Green Lake is not green, and there is no lake. The camp is actually in the middle of a desert. Thus, Sachar is kind of winking at the reader and whispering, "Hey, reader. Nothing in the book will be what it seems to be. Sachar winks at the reader many more times in the novel, using ironic names and titles to create reversals that flummox reader expectations. Even the hero's name, the palindrome Stanley Yelnats, is a reversal. Like the set ting in *Hoot*, the setting in *Holes* is an integral part of the story, and it would not take place anywhere but in that specific locale.

My own novel, *Soul Enchilada*, is set in El Paso, which is a major border crossing. Borders are a theme of the novel. Borders between countries. Borders between cultures. Borders between the supernatural and the ordinary. Borders between who we are what we want to be and what people expect of us. It used those borders throughout the novel to deepen themes and to turn the setting into a character of its own. I was able to do that in the very first draft because I saw all these borders when I was sticky noting the plot.

So setting matters. The characters you generate are part of the place where they live. You can use photos, music, maps, and anything that reminds you of a setting. Set them aside for later when you need to describe something, and just put a note on the sticky note wall to remind you that they exist. For example, don't tape a picture of a Victorian house on the sticky board. Just use the Sharpie to write "Victorian house" on a sticky and put it where the reader will see the house for the first time. As you post sticky notes, keep the setting in mind. Literally walk a mile in the hero's shoes and keep track of it with stickies.

During the first draft, it's often difficult to know all of the components of the story and to arrange those components to get the most effect from each element. There are links between character and setting, between setting and plot, and between plot and theme. There are also links to character and theme, as well as to character and setting. All of these elements are interlinked. Using a traditional writing process, a writer has to write many drafts to draw out those links. With the Sticky Note Plot method, we can iso late some of those important elements and then use the Sticky Note Plotting techniques to integrate them into the story from the very beginning. It saves time. It saves sanity.

When I first began brainstorming *Soul Enchilada*, I did not have a setting in mind. I had a main character, and I knew that main character delivered pizzas down windy roads. I wanted more from the setting than just a windy mountain road. I wanted a set ting that had a rich history as well as some kind of conflict embedded in its own story. So while I was sticky noting, I was jotting down the names of cities where the story could take place. Just off the top of my head, I came up with maybe two dozen cities. Onto the sticky note wall they went. El Paso was not one of those two dozen cities. But after researching those initial places, I found that none of them had a backstory that resonated with my main character. So I kept looking.

A few hours later, I learned that El Paso is both near a windy mountain and a border between Mexico and the United States. That border is always a source of conflict, and El Paso has a rich history as a West Texas town. El Paso! Yes! Onto the sticky note wall El Paso went. In a flurry of scribbling, I stickied more and more details about the town. There were so many details that I began to see patterns and themes emerging. At that point, it was easy then for me to build on those patterns and to strengthen the themes. As I moved throughout the Sticky Note Plot process, El Paso was always on my mind, a constant reminder to me to connect setting, characters, plot, and theme whenever possible. If I had tried to add those details after the novel was typed out on the page, it would have made the whole process much more difficult. I doubt that I would have been able to weave characterization, plot, setting, and theme together as effectively.

CHARACTERS IN DEPTH: KEY SCENES AND CHARACTER DEVELOPMENT

Once the setting is part of the plot, it's time to explore the characters in depth (Chapter 3), and after that, to identify the Key Scenes (Chapter 4), which are the essential scenes in the plot structure. Some writing gurus call them tentpoles. That visual doesn't work for me. It feels singular of purpose, and Key Scenes do a lot more than prop up the story.

Once you generate 60–80 stickies, and the story structure quadrants have roughly the same number of scenes, you can step back and fill in the gaps of the story. For some writers, those gaps bring doubts. When they say that their story is missing some important elements, they may wonder if those elements are necessary. Beyond the question about needing a villain, I'm often asked if a story really needs secondary characters with their own story arcs. No, it's not essential that secondary characters have their own story arcs. There are published novels whose secondary characters are only fillers. I'm also asked if a novel really needs Key Scenes. Does the story have to include every Key Scene? No. Can you write a successful novel without Key Scenes? Yes. Is life easier if you include Key Scenes? Absolutely!

No matter where you are on the writing career path—a first-time novelist or a mid-lister looking to break out, you want to make all the hard stuff easier. Experimentation is fine. None of us wants to get stuck in a rut. But be careful not to experiment so much that the story loses form and becomes too hard to finish. You want to write a first draft as easily as possible, so go with the techniques that worked for the giants that came before us.

ACTIVITIES
DIGGING DEEPER

The subconscious mind is a wondrous thing. Like elves in the shoemaker's shop, it will unknot story problems while you're off doing the dishes, washing the dog, pulling weeds, or watching the kids' game. It works especially hard while you're sleeping.

- Your subconscious is the secret sauce of the Sticky Note method, and all it needs is time. That's why we give the plot time to marinate. Like Diana Ross almost said, you can't hurry, bruh.
- Sure, if there's a burst of creativity and the ideas are flowing, you can and should slap stickies on the wall as fast as you can. Scribble on!
- Even after a flurry of scribbles, ideas will still be flowing, but more slowly. Soon, they will stop, and you may feel the need to forge ahead. Fight that feeling. I've found that when writers push at this point, they fall back on tropes, cliches, and easy answers.
- Leave the plot wall up for a week...or weeks. Let your subconscious make connections, sort through

possibilities, and find creative answers to hard questions. Prepare for epiphanies when you least expect them.

- Remember, a healthy Sticky Note Wall will have 6080 stickies. If you're in a hurry to get started writing before reaching that point, then you're probably starting too soon. Try to defer the desire to begin. Focus that energy on completing the wall. The creative energy will wait for you.

EXERCISE 1

Let's say you've been working on the wall for a couple weeks, and although you're pretty happy with the results, there are still some holes in the plot. Your reliable sub conscious is taking a break, and you're fresh out of ideas. Remember that group of writer friends? While they are still gathered, grab one of the sticky notes from another writer's wall and stick in a random spot on your own Wall (I call this Pin the Tail on the Novel). Then put one of your own stickies in the blank spot on their wall. Now, brainstorm how the borrowed sticky can become a plot point in the novel. PS. Don't give the sticky back and don't try to recover the one you gave away.

EXERCISE 2

Gather a group of writer friends and their Sticky Note Walls. Over snacks and drinks, each of you talk through the plots, highlighting the Key Scenes while the others ask clarifying questions about motivation, backstory, etc. It's a fun alternative to the traditional critique group.

STICKY NOTE CHECKLIST: THE STICKY NOTE PLOT

- Sticky chart paper pads can be expensive, but the sheets can be reused many times. One pack will last through dozens of plotting sessions.
- Use a Sharpie, not a pen. You need to be able to read the writing from several feet away. Using a Sharpie also prevents you from writing too much on a sticky, which is really a thing. Keep it short.
- We all have "that person" in our lives. You know, the well-meaning one who starts sentences with "I know what your novel really needs." Don't show the Sticky Note Wall to that person. A new story is a delicate thing. Protect it until it's stronger.
- Sticky Note Plotting is all about saying yes, even to weird ideas. In fact, the weirder, the better. Turn the internal editor off and say yes to everything. If you go down a rabbit hole, just throw the holey stickies away. It's easy to backtrack and start a new strand.

Exercise 2

Think about the premise of a current work in progress. Is the premise a cool idea? A unique twist on an old trope? A dilemma for the hero? Most importantly, is it about a main character in the novel? If it is, how can you make the premise more personal for the character? If it's not about a character but about the plot, how can you tweak the premise so that its outcomes affect the hero or another main character? How does the premise affect the hero's beliefs and misbeliefs?

Exercise 3

In this chapter, I described the Turn as the hinge on a compact (or a clamshell). Draw a picture of the compact. Label the left side "2A" and the right side "2B." List a few positive characteristics of the hero on the left. On the right, list the negative opposite of those characteristics. What could happen at the Turn that would make the hero change characteristics from positive to negative?

Sticky Note Checklist: Why Use Structure?

- To give you a clothesline to hang your story laundry.
- To tap into the collective unconsciousness of reader expectations.
- To avoid the twin curse of "too quiet" and "too episodic."
- To prevent you from ever having to ask the question, "okay, what the &%#$ happens now?" when you write yourself off the cliff at page one hundred.
- To preempt the dreaded "???" that beta readers scribble all over the margins when they can't figure out why in the world the characters would ever do such a thing.
- To ditch that panicked feeling when the little voice inside you says, "It's okay, no one will notice that the book abruptly ends in the last ten pages."
- To sell the manuscript to a publisher who just can't put it down.

PART 2

STICKY NOTING IT OUT

CHAPTER 3
CHARACTERS

WHEN I'M ASKED, "WHICH IS MORE IMPORTANT, plot or character?" my answer is always the same: Yes.

Plot is the net result of the decisions a character makes and the actions they take based on those decisions. It is impossible to separate character from plot, but that doesn't stop folks from trying to do so over and over again. Usually, we think of a plot as an outlining exercise, but I've worked with writers who try to outline their characters in advance. They do this by using character building worksheets.

In my experience, character worksheets are a dime a dozen, and that's about what they're worth. They are the swipe left of the novel craft world. Okay, I'll admit that character worksheets can be somewhat useful. They help you keep track of character details as you write the story. In the throes of the creative process, it's easy to forget things like the color of characters' eyes, their birthplaces, the length and color of their hair, and even their names. Somebody's got to keep track of all that stuff—that someone is you—so a worksheet record can be a lifesaver. It sure beats searching through two hundred plus pages trying to find where a blonde suddenly grows jet black hair or where a server named Loretta suddenly becomes Mavis. If you are prone to forgetting details like which country the story is set in, planning sheets keep track of these things.

But for truly creating heroes that a reader loves, cheers for, and wants to date in a parasocial way, worksheets won't cut it. They are fine for compiling character details but not for generating characters. We need to make our characters come alive, and the best way I know to do that is to plot the novel.

Yes, to plot the novel.

When I describe how to use the Sticky Note Plot to create the actions and events of the novel, I'm describing the crucial moments in the character's development. We often say that a character arc runs throughout the story. Arc is something of a misnomer. It implies that it's like McDonald's golden arches, aka it starts low, goes high, and then goes down. Characters will have highs and lows all the way through the novel. The character will feel as if they have accomplished something yet might later plunge into the depths of despair because they have not understood what's going on in their world.

CHARACTER IS PLOT, AND PLOT IS CHARACTER

Wait just a minute, you might be thinking, why is a craft book about plot starting with character? Because **character is plot, and plot is character**. The two can't be separated. So the age-old question of "which is more important, character or plot" is akin to asking, "which is more important, bones or muscles." Neither works without the other. There are many different moving parts to developing characters. Some people enjoy funny characters. Some people enjoy quirky ones. Some enjoy off-the-wall ones, and some enjoy just plain, ordinary people. Some people want to see themselves in the characters they read about. Others want to understand the world through another person's point-of-view.

None of that matters to you as a writer. What matters is that you understand why your characters do what they do. If you know that, then the reader will find what they're looking for in your novel. That's why we are going to delve into what makes a dynamic character before we try the Sticky Note Plot process.

Let's look at the first scene in any given story, which we call **The World As It Is**. The scene is not really about the world. It's about the world the character lives in. It's how comfortable they are, where they are in time and place. The setting really isn't Springfield, Illinois, but exactly where Eula May Ueker lives in Springfield, Illinois. It's in their house, in their neighborhood, in their home. The World As It Is scene is an essential one, and it's not wise to skip it. The World As It Is creates a beginning space for the reader. You're going to break/destroy/turn that world upside down, and the reader needs to get a glimpse of the hero's world as it is to truly understand what has been lost when the breaking happens.

THE AGITATION: STIRRING THE CONFLICT POT

When the world turns upside down, it causes the hero to respond. The hero's response is what I call the **Agitation**. The word Agitation can mean "a state of anxiety or nervous excitement," but in this case, I'm using it because of the second definition, "the action of briskly stirring or disturbing something." In other words, the author is stirring the pot—with gusto.

The Agitation compels the hero to respond to the change in the world. The story happens to the character, either directly or indirectly, so the Agitation has to have meaning for the character. Events that happen outside the character's world can have an effect on the character, but they react to it for reasons that are unique to them. The reaction to the Agitation is what leads to the Call to Action.

CALL TO ACTION: YOU NEED A HERO

The Call to Action is a demand for the hero to act. We have to understand something about the hero to understand why they would even think about acting. Many people when given a challenge to save the world or to even save a pizza won't accept that challenge. They're not up to the fight. The hero may be reluctant—for a variety of very good reasons—to take up the fight, but they will eventually because that's the kind of person they are (and the kind of person we want to be, which is why we're reading the book in the first place). There needs to be something in the hero's background that makes them willing to take up the fight, a fight that has to be meaningful to them.

Once the hero accepts the Challenge and begins their (metaphorical or literal) journey, we need to understand something about their lives and what's going on both in the world and inside the hero. For a character to become fully realized on the page, they must have wants and desires. There must be an underlying reason that they do what they do. Their actions have to matter to them, and if the actions matter to them, they will matter to the readers.

The best way I know to make plot matter is to dig into the hero's background. This digging is not a psychological examination of why they do what they do. We aren't Freud, and nobody wants to read a therapy session. This is not the hero's lifelong history. Nobody's life is that interesting, even James Bond's. This is an understanding of events in the past that have direct consequences on the hero's behavior in the fictive present. By the fictive present, I mean the stuff that's happening. Not in the previous chapter, not in the chapter ahead. Right now, on this very page where the action is occurring.

I can think of many different examples of characters who have acted in a certain way in their present because of things that happened to them BTB (Before the Book). There may be a hero who is afraid of commitment because they were abandoned at age six. Because they are afraid of commitment, they refuse to accept the

Call. There may be another hero who lost a dear family member to illness, so when one of their friends becomes sick, they run away, refusing to help out. There may be a hero who has a terrible temper and has been in many fights in their life and now is ordered by a judge to never be in another fight.

But when they and a friend are approached by a bully, they refuse to protect themselves, you understand exactly why they refuse to act. What is a huge act of self-restraint could easily be interpreted by the reader—and the hero's friend—as an act of cowardice. When creating characters, especially when they face dilemmas, context is everything.

BUILDING BACKSTORY: THE FOUNDATION FOR CHARACTER MOTIVATION

Okay, you may be thinking, that's all good for them, but how do I get my hero to that point? What are some techniques for developing meaningful characters with a depth of understanding? This is where backstory comes into play. Backstory doesn't have much of a role at the beginning of a novel. That's because too much background information about the character will bog down the reader. Just like too much worldbuilding will stop the world from coming alive. As the novel progresses, the reader will want to know more and more about the hero to understand what they do.

One writer who is adept at building backstory while the plot unfolds is Carl Hiaasen. Hiaasen knows how to hide large chunks of backstory early on in a novel, and he's done it with both novels for adults and for children. He uses a variety of techniques to pull it off. Sometimes, he parcels backstory out between paragraphs. He will insert one or two sentences between a couple of longer paragraphs to sprinkle in details about the hero's past. Hiaasen tends to break chapters into three separate scenes. He'll write one or two scenes at the beginning of the chapter that are happening in the fictive present. Then he will insert a time jump between the second and third scenes. During that time jump, he will insert a healthy chunk of backstory, sometimes up to a thousand words.

The chunk of backstory Hiaasen inserts isn't just there for window dressing—it relates directly to the events in the upcoming scene. He explicates the background of the character and also lets the reader understand the motivation for how the character is going to act next. For example, his novel Hoot opens with a chapter about the hero, who is riding the bus to school. Out the window, he sees a shirtless boy running past the school bus and into the woods. During the scene, Hiaasen parcels out bits of backstory about Dana's previous life—his family has just moved to Florida from Montana, and his feeling like the proverbial fish out of water. The reader needs to know this information to show Roy's state of mind.

What the reader doesn't need is a chunk of exposition about Roy's life up to this point or an internal monologue about past traumatic events in Montana. Those details are unnecessary for the action of the scene, so the reader doesn't need to know that information.

Once the action of the story is humming along, Hiaasen hits the expository pause button after the opening scene of the chapter. Here, he drops a long bit of exposition, over three hundred words, that goes into detail about Roy's birthplace and later home. This information is crucial to the next few scenes. Without it, the reader wouldn't understand his interaction with other characters. While a chunk of exposition this long would have been death to the action in the opening scene of the novel, Hiaasen allowed the momentum of the story to build before he tucked Roy's exposition neatly between two scenes.

The key to writing an effective backstory is the reader only what they need to understand the current scene. Good backstory deepens character development in this scene. Bad backstory is just an info dump that either won't matter until later in the novel or never really matters at all. Hiaasen's technique allows the reader to process the events of the previous chapter while finding out more about the hero, right before the scene makes use of that information. It makes the reader feel in the know. It makes the reader feel smart. It's much better when the reader feels smart than when the reader feels dumb. The more the character has a variety of past experiences, the more you can use those experiences to inform what the characters are doing now and to provide the human element that's often missing from first drafts: Motivation.

HURTING YOUR CHARACTERS: BUILDING EMPATHY WITH THE READER

Motivation helps us understand why characters take certain actions. If beta readers say that the hero does things for no reason or worse, that the hero does things because the plot needs them to, then you may have a problem with motivation. So how do we really show the reader the hero's motivation? How do we create a strong reader/character bond that allows the reader to understand the heroes and care deeply about them? The answer is simple:

Hurt them.

Hurt them so good.

Now that the song is stuck in your head, let me explain what I mean by that and why it's so effective. I want you to damage the heroes so that they grow stronger and so that their connections to readers grow stronger. We always hurt the ones we love...because they deserve it.

Just kidding.

But not really.

There are lots of methods for hurting the characters. Take them out of their homes. Take away their families. Break their hearts. Kill their parents. Cut off their hands. How far are you willing to go? Probably not far enough. This section, though, isn't really about convincing you to hurt the characters or about giving you creative ways to do it. You're brilliant, so you can think of much more dastardly ways to hurt the hero than I can.

According to Helen Keller, character can't "be developed in ease and quiet. Only through experience of trial and suffering can the soul be strengthened, ambition inspired, and success achieved." In other words, you go on summer vacation with your parents and four siblings in a station wagon. Even better, in a station wagon with zero air conditioning during the hottest August on record. Does that feel sadistic? Kurt Vonnegut said writers are supposed to be sadists.

We, however, don't want it to be mean. We're nice people. We love our characters. How many of us have smiled at a first kiss we wrote? How many of us have cried over when those lovers broke up, even though the relationship only ever existed in our own heads? How many of us have choked up over a poignant moment that formed as we typed? How many of us have mourned the deaths of our imaginary friends?

Raise your hand.

If you didn't raise your hand, you better put it up, so people won't know you're heartless. Heartless writers don't get very far. Neither do overly kind ones.

There are psychological reasons we don't want to hurt our heroes. The reasons have a great deal to do with how we as human beings interact with one another. It is a thing we call empathy, and because we actually are kindhearted sadists, we are going to examine how to take advantage of it.

MIRROR NEURONS AND MONKEY BUSINESS: WHY WE WANT WHAT THE OTHER GUY HAS

According to neuroscientist Giacomo Rizzolatti, the act of reading and listening actually stimulates the same part of the brain that fires when we are feeling empathy, an area known as mirror neurons. Our mirror neurons help us understand the actions of others and prime us to imitate the experience, including experiences that we are reading about.

While Rizzolatti's researchers haven't been able to find a specific motor neuron in humans, they have learned that humans have an empathetic response to other humans. When we see people in danger, our empathy region grows larger and larger.

The human brain cannot distinguish between felt and read emotions. It feels through an initial behavior. When challenged to distinguish felt emotions from those described in fiction, it cannot do so. In some ways, the brain is more active when reading a story than experiencing the original stimulus itself.

The next question is, if we are so empathetic as human beings and if writing and reading fires that same part of our brain as our lived experiences, why should we hurt characters?

The answer is, so that readers feel a strong emotional connection to characters. That emotional response can in turn become a physiological attachment. That's because when we feel that emotion in our brains, the same chemical that encourages a bond between people who have experienced, say a traumatic event or couples who are intimate, it's the same chemical. So reading a book recreates the same addictive physiological response as the actual event. Knowing this allows writers to create a phenomenon called parasocial relationships.

CHARACTERS AND PARASOCIAL RELATIONSHIPS: IT'S NOT ALL IN YOUR HEAD

Parasocial interaction is defined as "a relationship that a person imagines having with another person whom they do not actually know, such as a celebrity or a fictional character." Parasocial interaction was first described from the perspective of media and communication studies. In 1956, two researchers, Donald Horton and Richard Wohl, explored the different interactions between mass media users and media figures, aka watching daytime dramas, or what my Grandma Gill used to call "her stories." Soap operas made us realize the power of a parasocial relationship, which is when users act as if they're involved in the typical social relationships being portrayed on screen.

Soap operas during the 1950s and 60s were always about doctors and lawyers, not because there was anything exciting about the doctors and lawyers themselves but because the life and death nature of medicine and law gave TV writers instantly powerful dramatic situations that were eminently filmable.

Housewives, a class of people created in large part in the patriarchal aftermath of WWII, watched every day and became addicted to the stories. Moreover, because stay at home wives may have felt more isolated than the previous generation, they felt lonelier and more stranded in their own homes. They formed relationships with the daily television characters. They often had discussions with their real-life friends and loved ones about soap opera characters as if they were real things.

My grandma would often bring up a character who needed surgery as if the person was real. This perplexed my dad, who asked if the person was real or made up before he would listen to her concerns. But for my grandma, who lived alone, the characters were very real, and they mattered. That's the takeaway for novelists: characters matter. Parasocial relationships enable us to explore emotional and social realities without the risks of the real world.

We are protected from the social rejection and physical danger of threatening circumstances, like forming a relationship with an interesting but potentially dangerous person. Thomas Shelby, for example, was a cool character on the BBC television series *Peaky Blinders*. Handsome. Debonaire. Self-assured and extremely brave. But he was also the leader of a criminal family, and you might not want to eat dinner with a ruthless murderer. In the real world, a friendship with him would present obstacles, but in the narrative world, those obstacles can disappear.

According to psychologist and author Jennifer Lynn Barnes, the parasocial relationships we have with real people operate very similarly to the relationships we have with fictional characters. Seeing a picture of a favorite fictional character can have what we call social facilitation effects, which we would normally see if we were in the presence of friends. Being "coupled" with your favorite character increases self-esteem and can make you feel a sense of belonging. We call this fandom.

As an author, you can incorporate the knowledge of parasocial relationships into the development of your characters. Because the reader is already "coupled," they will feel any stimulus that the character feels. The more powerful the stimulus, the more the reader bonds with the character. The most powerful stimulus I can think of is hurting the characters. Hurts can come in any shape or size, but for our purposes, I've divided them into three categories: physical, emotional, and transformational.

PHYSICAL HURTS: HOW TO SLOW YOUR HERO DOWN

Physical hurts can be small hurts. The hero can fall down. They could be cut. They can be tripped or pushed around. They can drop something heavy on their toe and have to go to urgent care to have their toenail taken off (if you winced at that image, it's because your mirror neurons just fired). There's a plethora of ways authors can cause small hurts that really don't affect character development or move the story along.

The following description contains a huge plot spoiler. It's from *The Queen of Attolia* by Megan Whelan Turner, the follow-up to the Newbery Honor, *The Thief*. In *The Thief*, Gen is a legendary thief who is so skilled at sleight of hand, he can steal anything from anybody, including the most precious treasure of a neighboring nation. In *Queen of Attolia*, Gen is caught spying on the queen of that neighboring nation. He expects to be hanged for his spying, but the queen instead cuts off his right hand, the punishment for being a thief.

Yes, cuts off his hand, which is absolutely essential to his craft.

Without the hand, he can't steal, and without the ability to steal, he loses his identity. He is no longer the Thief. He is no one. Maimed and heartbroken, Gen returns home and wallows in a deep depression.

The Queen of Attolia, surprisingly, regrets her actions, and that regret sets off a chain of events that not only change her and Gen, but almost cause a war. Believe it or not, the amputation was an act of love. You have to read the novels to see why.

Maiming a wildly popular and successful character took great courage from the author. Turner's decision may not have made her editor happy initially, but it allowed Gen to grow, change, and mature in a way that he never would have been able to initially. It also allowed the queen to show remorse, something she was incapable of in the first book of the series.

EMOTIONAL HURTS: HOW TO HURT YOUR HERO FROM THE INSIDE

So let's amp it up. Let's turn those small hurts into big hurts. Hurts are bigger if they are emotional. Like bodily injuries, emotional injuries that are important to the story engage the reader at a visceral, empathetic level. And they also turn a backstory from a handy bit of exposition into past trauma that shapes the hero's current behavior and may lead to poor choices. Emotional hurts are bigger than physical hurts, but they don't really change the arc of the novel.

The next novel I'm going to spoil is *See You at Harry's* by Jo Knowles. It tells the story of twelve-year-old Fern who, although she feels invisible, has too much going on in her life. Fern's older sister has no clear plan for life. Fern's older brother doesn't know how to come out about his sexual orientation to his family. Fern's parents are holding the family restaurant together, too busy to notice Fern. Fern is even overshadowed by her younger brother Charlie, whose infectious laughter and unbridled joy is the glue that holds the family together. Fern's life putters along like this until the midpoint of the book: Charlie is injured while under Fern's care, and although no one knows it at the time, his injuries lead to his death. The whole family is devastated. They become so lost in their own grief, they forget about Fern, who is paralyzed by both grief and guilt.

This transformation scene works at both the physical and emotional levels. Not only does a child die (which one reviewer said it made her sob so uncontrollably, she could barely breathe), Fern is left alone to deal with a tragedy, which is horribly unfair and triggers our desire to make right the wrongs she's feeling.

TRANSFORMATIONAL HURTS AND THE BIG HURT COMBO: FOR THE WIN

Transformational hurts are so profound, so essential to the fabric of the story that they must change the character (and the plot) permanently. The damage done to the character transforms the character and then transforms the story around them. Transformational hurts occur with the violation of a societal norm which leads to a miscarriage of justice. Most heroes—and readers—have a strong sense of justice. The transgression transforms the hero from someone who acts on their self-interest to a righteous crusader who is determined to right a wrong. Readers love that.

Of all the types of hurt that we have in our society, we may be really hardwired for one in particular. Humans have an ingrained sense of fair play. So do other animals, suggesting that the desire for justice and fair play is not limited to human beings. Dogs, for example, can pout if another dog gets more food, and Capuchin monkeys get downright violent if they see another monkey receive grapes when they themselves were fed cucumber.

Another spoiler: In *The Hunger Games* by Suzanne Collins, the hero is Katniss Everdeen. At the beginning of the novel, Katniss sacrifices her own wellbeing by volunteering to enter the hunger games in her sister's place. While she's training, Katniss makes almost no friends, but the one friend she does make is with a young girl named

Rue. Rue is completely ill-suited to be in the Hunger Games. She is young and small, and although she has some skill, it is obvious that she will be overmatched.

Always a champion for the underdog, Katniss quickly bonds with Rue. When they are in the arena, Katniss protects the young girl as best she can, but the competition takes its toll. Rue is killed, and Katniss is the one who finds her body. In a devastatingly emotional scene, Katniss gives Rue an impromptu funeral, and she turns the moment into an act of defiance against the Capitol, which is forcing teens into competing in a series of deadly survivor games.

If I were using sticky notes to plot out this scene, I would jot down notes about three different aspects of the action—physical, emotional, and transformational. That's part of the beauty of using the Sticky Note Plot method. You aren't limited to the action. You can delve into the motivation and psychological state of the hero. Using sticky notes to do this work at the beginning save time and rewriting.

In *Hunger Games*, the scene with Rue works on several levels. It works on a physical level because Rue dies. It works on an emotional level, not only because Katniss loses her friend, but because Rue is a surrogate for Katniss' sister Prim, for whom she sacrificed herself and entered the arena. It works on a transformational level because Rue's death becomes a rallying cry that will eventually overthrow the Capitol. In a single scene, Katniss' act of kindness and defiance becomes the pivotal point of the entire series. How would you know that a scene like this was necessary? In a traditionally written first draft, you might not know, but if saw the scene using the Sticky Note Plot, you would recognize its importance quickly and sub consciously tweak previous scenes to lead up to that incredibly dramatic moment.

THE BIG COMBO HURT: LET LOOSE THE MONSTERS

If you really want to create a lasting parasocial bond between the hero and the reader, you've got to go for the Big Hurt Combo (BHC). You can employ the BHC by combining physical, emotional, and transformational hurts so that their personal hurt affects the larger story world simultaneously, then you have truly damaged the hero. The damage will make the reader so, so sad and make you, dear author, so, so happy.

Sometimes to create sympathy for our characters, we have to turn the monsters loose. We need to see how the protagonist will respond to the monsters. No matter what shape they take, real or imagined, no matter what the hero faces, the reader must never give up hope that the hero will succeed. As Anne Lamott says, "there is no point in writing hopeless novels. We all know we're going to die. What's important is the kind of men and women we are in the face of this." The question is how do you make the reader care? How do you encourage them to feel empathy for the characters? How do you fire off those chemicals in their brain?

My suggestion? Give them someone they can love immediately.

I have a dog named Moose. He is a Nova Scotia Duck Tolling Retriever. To know him is to love him. Picture a smaller golden retriever with a pink nose, a sweeping tail, keen intelligence, and eyes full of mischief. As a hunting dog, he was bred to be adorable, hyperactive, and loud. My eldest daughter adopted him from the pound while she was in college, so he lived with me and eventually became my dog. Although he is purebred, his breeder turned him in to the pound due to his jacked up but hilarious underbite and a slight hip dysplasia, which made him unsuitable for showing.

Did I tell you that Moose is smart? Moose can spell. Like most dogs, if you say the word "walk" around him, he will lose his mind. So I started avoiding the word by spelling it. Moose figured that out quick. He also generalized that other words such as jog, stroll, and excursion meant walk. He is not fooled by the words waffle or wallet, which don't even cause his eyes to twitch.

Moose is definitely getting his own place on the wall. So I scribble out these details on several stickies: Smart dog. Playful and curious. Golden colored with a swishy tail. Can speak English. May have a protective side that comes out in times of danger.

After hearing about Moose, would you care if Moose ran away? Would you care if he were stolen? Would you have more empathy for me as his owner or my daughter as his rescuer? What if Moose were intentionally killed? Would you have even more empathy? What if my daughter's enemy killed Moose? How would you feel about the enemy? Why would you think about the enemy if that happened? Would you take pleasure in seeing them painfully pay for his crime?

Yes, you would. These questions go onto stickies, and those stickies go on the wall, even if I don't know exactly where to put them. I can always move them later.

Right now you're probably thinking less of me for even suggesting the idea of hurting Moose. Just to be clear, I will never harm Moose. But we, as writers, have to be willing to go there. We have to be willing to think about it. And at times we have to be willing to write about it.

ACTIVITIES
DIGGING DEEPER

Some writers have a difficult time with the concept of hurting characters, even after hearing all of the valid reasons for doing so. It is, I believe, because they have for med parasocial relationships with their own characters, echoing the Greek myth of Pygmalion, who created a statue so beautiful, he fell in love with it. The myth lent a title to George Bernard Shaw's play *Pygmalion*, which in turn was adapted as the Broadway musical *My Fair Lady*. As Henry Higgins learns, falling in love with your own creation leads to heartache.

- If you're unable to hurt the hero, ask yourself if it is the case only for this character. Are you able to hurt other characters? Can you think of bad things to do to the villain?
- If so, then you can probably get around the idea of protecting the hero. Just pretend that they dumped you for another author! Okay, I'm not serious. Well, kind of serious.
- If you're unable to hurt any characters, you may be one of those writers who avoids conflict at all costs. That's going

to make the writing life really hard but maybe not impossible. In my experience, it's physical harm that conflict-avoidant authors don't like.

- Concentrate on the other ways to do hurts, especially Transformational Hurts on a huge scale. Somehow, dropping a meteor on Los Angeles feels less personal than cutting off your imaginary heartthrob's hand.

EXERCISE 1

In real life, we despair when things go from bad to worse. In a novel, when the going gets rough, we are on the edge of our seats, dying to find out what happens next. Pick a scene on your Sticky Note Wall (see Chapter 4) where things are going badly for the hero. Make them worse. Take away their money. Have their car break down and strand them on a desert highway. Cause a blackout and have all their food in the fridge go bad. Break a leg. Cut off a limb. Now pick three more scenes and do the same thing.

EXERCISE 2

Sometimes you can hurt the hero indirectly by making things go well for the characters that oppose them. The obvious choice is the villain, but it can be any character who wants the same thing the hero does. Pick five places on the Sticky Note Wall where things are going well for an antagonist and reward them heavily. Be like anti-Santa— give presents to the bad list children. Make sure that the gifts they receive will be used against the hero in some way.

EXERCISE 3

Although they are effective, Big Hurt Combos are difficult to create. Multiple parts of the story have to come together, and when you're generating a Sticky Note Wall, most of those parts don't exist yet.

This is especially true (for me) of Emotional Hurts because they derive from character development. One way to bring Emotional Hurts into existence is to build backstory. Not just any backstory. The backstory of a physical hurt. Pick a spot on the Sticky Note Wall where a character gets hurt. Scribble out a couple of lines about when they have been hurt before and by whom. The old who, what, when, where, and how. Put the backstory sticky underneath the physical hurt sticky and pick two other stickies to create backstory for. Bonus points if you do it at the Turn.

STICKY NOTE CHECKLIST: CHARACTERS

- Plot is the net result of the decisions a character makes and the actions they take based on those decisions.
- It is impossible to separate character from plot.
- Character is plot, and plot is character.
- Motivation helps us understand why characters do what they do. If beta readers complain about the characters, it's probably because there is a lack of motivation. Backstory is a good way to show motivation.
- Hurting characters builds empathy. Empathy engages the reader's brain and strengthens the connection between them and the characters.
- Heroes are heroic. They overcome things that we can't. The key word is overcome. It's not enough to place obstacles in front of them if those obstacles are easily overcome. We want to see heroes work for it.

CHAPTER 4
KEY SCENES

A S I MENTIONED EARLIER, Key Scenes are important scenes that serve as the support structure of the protagonist's character arc. They are all about the hero—what they know, do, feel, remember, and decide. Key scenes are so important that they are as close to essential as any plot elements that I describe in this book. It is very difficult to develop a well-rounded, active hero without them. With that in mind, let's talk about the Key Scenes and why they are so important. Grab some stickies, and let's create a plot!

WORLD AS IT IS, INCITING EVENT, CHALLENGE MADE, AND CHALLENGE ACCEPTED

For the purpose of the Sticky Note Plotting exercise, I recommend doing the stickies that establish the **World As It Is** first, so that it is the very first note that you stick on the wall. Why? Because you are building a world for your own imagination to inhabit. So grab a stickie. Write, World As It Is on it, and stick it on the wall. Some folks start their walls with character details, which is fine, but I start mine with setting. Setting is the deep background of the story, and it helps me put parameters on my imagination.

Here, I scribble out bits of setting: time, place, history, population, geography, power structures, and other unique qualities that add nuance or intrigue to the plot. The setting of the story establishes everything that follows. We want the reader to be grounded in time and place, so you must ground yourself in time and place, as well. Often, setting stickies can overwhelm the others in the first act, as you get flashes of inspiration for all the intricate details of the setting. Instead of spreading all of these stickies out, stack them on top of each other. This will allow you to build an idea sandbox but won't overwhelm the rest of the plotting space.

Don't want to generate setting details first? No problem! Whatever path you take to starting a sticky note wall is good. However, once you've slapped a few dozen stickies on the wall, take a step back, take a breath, and start rearranging the stickies so that all the World As It Is stickies are at the beginning of Act 1.

INCITING EVENT

In Act 1, once we have established the world, that world immediately changes. Remember what I wrote earlier about the old Wile E. Coyote and Roadrunner cartoons? There is a rock poised on the side of a cliff with a small stick holding it. That is the World As It Is. The Road Runner runs by and trips a wire. This stick is released, and the ball starts rolling. That ball is the **Inciting Event**. Once the ball starts rolling, it cannot be stopped, and that is the same thing you need from the inciting event in Act 1. When you do the sticky for this Key Scene, you can only use one note. The Inciting Event is a single event. It's not a sequence of events, and it is not something you can spread thinly over the span of Act 1. One sticky. That's all. Don't stack multiple stickies atop each other. Write only the words needed to establish the one specific moment that starts the ball rolling with so much momentum, nothing can stop it. This poses a challenge to the fictive world and more importantly to your hero.

CHALLENGE ACCEPTED

Near the end of Act 1, there is a Key Scene that is ubiquitous in modern novels. It's where the hero accepts the responsibility and begins a new journey. This comes directly out of Joseph Campbell, but remember, Campbell's work is descriptive of the stories he read. It's not a prescription for writing a novel. Structurally, though, there's a reason that the journey happens at this point. Where does the Challenge come from? Most likely, it comes from the Inciting Event and its immediate fallout. It can come from other places, too. Where? Your imagination will tell you. On a sticky, write down reasons your hero would be challenged, one reason per sticky. Put them on the wall. The first couple of ideas might work. Or they might be the most obvious reason, ones that depend on tropes rather than character development. Keep scribbling. Think divergently. Put all the ideas on the wall, and avoid thinking, "That's stupid," and tossing out-there ideas. Sometimes, those are the best ideas of all.

The **Challenge Accepted** scene is more than just the hero saying, "Yes, I will slay your dragon/run that marathon/solve this case/ask someone out on a date." The acceptance of the challenge creates a foundation for the end of Act 1 and the beginning of Act 2. In Act 2A, the hero begins the Hero's Journey, which will begin with them accepting responsibility, whatever that responsibility may be. Unlike the Inciting Event, which is a very specific event in the story, The Challenge Accepted scenes can happen any time after the Inciting Event.

You will use lots of stickies in this phase. Maybe you write a sticky that the hero refuses the challenge at first. A reluctant hero is not a bad hero, but it certainly raises conflict and stakes if the hero isn't completely sold on being a hero. Other characters may have to talk them into it. Which characters? Write their names and reasons on stickies. Put them on the wall. Is conflict created during this phase? Write the conflicts on a sticky, too!

JOURNEY BEGINS, THE HERO'S MONTAGE, BUILDING BRIDGES, AND FALSE VICTORY

Once the hero has accepted the challenge, they must go forward on their journey. These are my favorite stickies to generate! They are so much fun. Because I learned so much about my hero and other characters in plotting Act 1, I get very specific story ideas. The more specific the idea, I've found, the easier it will be to write later. When you generate stickies at this point, you may slow down. The ideas may not come flying from the left and right of your brain. That's perfectly fine. I always slow down here. It's because of that specificity. I want to grab the details, rather than the big ideas. There will be time for more big ideas later.

Just to clarify: a Hero's Journey can be many things. It can be a literal journey or a short quest. It may be a metaphorical journey in which the hero doesn't even leave town. It may also be as simple as the hero following their desire line in a typical high school classroom. The journey can be a sweeping epic, or it can be small and important to only one character. It doesn't matter, as long as it starts. Like the Challenge Accepted, the **Journey Begins** Key Scene can happen over a period of scenes, rather than being one crystallized moment in the story. The hero can be packing up, preparing, procrastinating, etc. You decide what preparations are needed. But do start the journey. Get the hero to pursue a clear and well-defined goal. A goal that you will, of course, scribble down and put on the wall.

THE HERO'S MONTAGE

Once the journey starts, the hero has a series of small victories. If they are learning to fight, the **Hero's Montage** is made of the scenes where they go from a novice warrior to the deadliest warrior in the tribe. Think Wonder Woman. Or if this is an 80s teen comedy, this is where our geeky hero learns how to dress for success or learns to dance their butt off like a maniac. These scenes are often light and fun because the hero is on a roll. Light and fun are magic words to Sticky Noters. Here's where you tap your inner child and get a little crazy. Throw all the stickies you can at this Key Scene. No idea is too silly, wild, absurd, or off the wall, as long as it seems inevitable that the hero will be able to reach their goal quickly and successfully. The key word again is *seems*.

FALSE VICTORY

The final scene of Act 2 is a **false victor**y—the hero looks like they will win, but the opposite is true. Up to this point, the hero has been journeying and has had some hardships, but generally has had a pretty easy go of it. However, they are about to fail when the stakes are high. That's a false victory. After the hero's False Victory, boom! Some terrible thing happens, and the false victory is wiped away by what happens next. Take a look at the wall you've built so far. Is there an obvious chance for a false victory? If so, jot it down. If not, and that's often the case, take a few minutes to ponder possibilities. Does anything pop into your head? Yes? That's awesome. Write it down. No? If you're drawing a blank here, don't worry about it. Ideas will come to you later, so skip over this part and move on to what I believe is the most important Key Scene of the novel.

THE TURN

The middle of a novel has often been called the midpoint, but the middle of the story needs to be more than just a halfway point. It needs to be a significant, irreversible alteration that the hero (and the reader) can't return from. In other words, a point of no return. Remember that I talked about **the Turn** being a traumatic event that happens *to* the novel. It can happen to the hero, one of the secondary characters, or to the world they live in. The event is something that dramatically changes the trajectory of the story. One or more characters are altered so that they are forever changed, and those changes catapult us through the rest of the story. A great Turn fixes the middle muddle. It makes Act 2B important and imperative. It compels the reader to keep reading.

When you first start plotting the novel, you probably won't know what the Turn will be, because the Turn is an event that destroys what you've created. You can't destroy what you've created until you've created it, so don't worry if you don't know the Turn to begin with. It will appear, as long as you're willing to make the hero and the people they love suffer greatly.

THE VILLAIN'S MONTAGE, SECOND JOURNEY, BURNING BRIDGES, AND FALSE DEFEAT

The Villain's Montage (which may cover several scenes): Now we move into Act 2B, which is the antithesis of Act 2A. Everything that went right in the hero's montage goes wrong in the villain's montage. This is where the stuff hits the fan, and there's nobody willing to clean it up.

After scheming in the background while the hero did their thing, the villain finally gets an opportunity to show his stuff. All along, the villain has been nurturing a hidden, secret plot to defeat the hero and to make their own dreams come true. They have been acting on their desire line, and now it is coming to fruition, even as the hero is suffering. Like the first montage and Act 2A, this montage can be a series of small victories for the antagonist. Generate as many ideas as you can. These don't have to be a specific scene that is firm in your mind at this point.

Second Journey: If the first journey was to a place, the **second journey** is away from a place. The hero is running, physically, emotionally, or metaphorically (can you do all three—I bet you can) away from the events of the Turn. Think of Acts 2B and 2A as the opposite sides of a coin, the villain's Yang to the hero's Yin. The antithesis to the thesis. These two parts of the Act are a mirror of one another. As the antagonist rises, the protagonist falls. Allowing the antagonist to take over Act 2B will make the second half of the story more bionic—stronger, faster, and much more thrilling.

BURNING BRIDGES

All of those relationships from Act 2A? They are toast. Except for maybe the most important one, and even that one is iffy. If there were physical bridges built in 2A, the antagonist has blown them up. Since many novels flounder during this part of the story, allowing the antagonist to take over the storyline will invigorate the reader and allow you to move us very quickly and organically into the Last Key Scene of Act 2B, the false defeat.

FALSE DEFEAT

Like there is a false victory at the end of Act 2A, there is a **False Defeat** at the end of Act 2B. It looks as if our character is down for the count. The antagonist is thrilled. Her plan of world domination is to the point of fruition. They have captured the hero and tied them to the nose cone of a ballistic missile, and they are prepared to send that missile into space, disrupting the space-time continuum and disposing of the hero at the same time.

The hero is done for. There is nothing they can do to escape. It seems as if everything they accomplished has turned on a dime, and the events of the Turn have come to fruition. They are utterly, completely defeated. But they are not dead yet. Because they still have to face the Dark Night of the Soul.

DARK NIGHT OF THE SOUL, NEW PLAN, TERRIBLE CHOICE, CHALLENGE COMPLETED, AND WORLD AS IT WILL BE

Dark Night of the Soul: Like the Inciting Event and Challenge Accepted, this Key Scene is found in many works of literature. It is the point where the character understands what a fool they have been, how their flaws have led them to this moment, and how they are utterly, completely defeated. They turn their newfound wisdom in on themselves, and they berate themselves mentally and possibly physically for the damage they have done because of their vanity or lack of understanding (aka the misbelief). This moment usually happens in the night because it truly is the darkest before the dawn. Thus, the name Dark Night of the Soul. Before the hero gives up completely, something happens, and they find hope.

The Dark Night is a single scene. It is the linchpin between Acts 2 and 3. The stronger this scene is, the better the final act is going to be. This is the ultimate Aftermath, the long aftermath of the false defeat where the hero struggles with failure, guilt, grief, loss, powerlessness, hubris, etc. Make it hurt.

NEW PLAN

When the dawn comes, the hero has made it through the crisis and is ready to act against the antagonist. If they have been imprisoned, their loyal friends break them out. If they have been in a prison of their own making, a sudden epiphany breaks them out. Once they are free, they are on a mission, and with the help of the friends who haven't given up on them, they make a plan. The **New Plan** is the engine that drives the story to the end.

SOPHIE'S CHOICE

This scene is optional. The idea behind the **Sophie's Choice** is that the hero must choose between two equally undesirable consequences. This technique takes its name from William Styron's novel, *Sophie's Choice*, in which Auschwitz survivor Sophie was forced to choose which of her two children would live and which would be gassed.

Not every Terrible Choice needs to be as horrible as choosing which of your children will die, but if you can create a dilemma for the character, the character will be significantly more sympathetic and heroic.

CHALLENGE COMPLETED

The New Plan worked! Using the relationship(s) they have created and the understanding of their own weaknesses, the hero acts. We follow them along as they make one right move after another, defeating any underlings the antagonist may have put between them. They may lose a few friends along the way, but they understand their greater purpose in the story. Eventually, there's a climactic scene with the antagonist and protagonist butting heads, and one of them wins. Life is easier if the hero wins. Most people don't want to read a novel about the bad guys winning. Think about *The Chocolate War*. The bad guy won, and readers are still angry 50 years later.

But in your novel, the hero wins, and the challenge that they accepted way back at the end of Act 1 is complete.

WORLD AS IT WILL BE

The story comes full circle. The new baseline is established. Change has occurred. The hero and their world will never be the same.

When you're doing the Sticky Note Plot, it will take a while to nail down the final sequence of Key Scenes. It is enough to know that you need a plan for the hero. You don't have to know the plan in great detail yet. Just do as many stickies as you can for the Key Scenes. The last act is an important place to consider possibilities. As Aristotle pointed out in Poetics, endings should be surprising "but the inevitable result of what has gone before."

And now the end is near. The equilibrium that was destroyed in the opening scene is returned. We go back to the way the world is supposed to be. Things are changed. The hero is changed. But the reader knows that it's going to be, even if they don't live happily ever after. As with Challenge Completed, a few notes are all you really need at this point.

So what are you waiting for? Let's finish the plot!

ACTIVITIES
DIGGING DEEPER

If you read enough craft books, you'll find the concept of Key Scenes in almost every one of them. Different authors will call them by different names and explain them using different terms.

Published in 1949, Campbell's *The Hero with a Thousand Faces* draws inspiration from Carl Jung's psychoanalytical theories to assemble a unified theory of narrative, which Campbell termed the monomyth. The monomyth, despite its name, is not universal. Campbell brought personal and cultural biases to the research, and those biases exclude other forms of story structure that do not fit a Western model that dates back to Aristotle and Greek theatre. The world is huge and complex with as many ways to tell stories as there are cultures. The Hero's Journey is just one way to structure stories. It certainly is not the only way.

In addition, the monomyth is not concerned with individual characters. Instead, it concentrates on character archetypes, which are character types that fit a group of instantly recognizable behaviors. Authors often make use of these archetypes, which include such common roles as Hero, Mentor, Ally, Herald, Trickster, Shapeshifter, Guardian, or Shadow. For example, in Star Wars, Obi-Wan is the

Mentor, Han Solo is the Shapeshifter, and R2D2 is the Trickster. Emperor Palpatine is the Shadow that looms over them all. Luke is, of course, the Hero. What characters in your novel could fit an archetype?

EXERCISE 1

Look at the characters on your Sticky Note Wall. Pick one that could fulfill the role of either Hero, Mentor, Ally, Herald, Trickster, Shapeshifter, Guardian, or Shadow. On a sticky note, list the personality traits and background that show that they fit the archetype.

EXERCISE 2

Star Wars is not the only film that uses the Hero's Journey as a template. Some critics have suggested many novels that follow the monomyth pattern, such as *On the Road*, *Silence of the Lambs*, *Of Mice and Men*, *Lord of the Rings*, and *The Notebook*. Pick two books from the list and Google the search phrase "novels that use Joseph Campbell's hero's journey" to find three more. Read at least three of the novels while taking notes on the hero's journey cycle. Do the novels really fit the cycle? How do they deviate from it? Do the changes make the story weaker or stronger?

STICKY NOTE CHECKLIST: KEY SCENES

- Key scenes are as close to essential as any plot elements described in this book.
- It is very difficult to develop a well-rounded, active hero without using Key Scenes.
- Start with the World As It Is when generating stickies to ground the story in time and place.

- The Inciting Event is a singular event. Don't stretch it out, or it may lose its impact.
- Conversely, Challenge Accepted can happen over several scenes.
- The Journey that starts Act 2A doesn't need to be a literal journey. It can be emotional, spiritual, personal, etc.
- In the Hero's Montage, the hero is often acting on their misbelief to build bridges. The misbelief will lead to their False Victory and will be revealed at the Turn.
- The Villain's Montage drives Act 2B, while it may not be apparent to the hero and their friends. The villain doesn't have to be the one to destroy bridges. A misguided hero will do it to themselves.
- The Dark Night of the Soul is one long Aftermath (see Chapter 8)
- The World As It Will Be shows both how the world has changed and how the hero changed it. If the hero's actions don't affect that change, then the story may not be about them.

PART 3

GENERATING A DRAFT

"The first draft is just you telling yourself the story."

—TERRY PRATCHETT

CHAPTER 5
GENERATING SCENES

AST CHAPTER, I TOLD YOU ABOUT KEY SCENES and how to put them on your wall. Now, I'm going to help you generate stickies to fill out the other scenes. Although they are not Key Scenes, they are essential to the story. Let's assume that you have decided to plot out the novel. You want to be able to work as efficiently as possible and brainstorm as easily as possible, but you still want to be able to capture that brainstorming and to later put it in (some kind of) order. Me too! Which I did, and this is the process that I developed over time.

THE STICKY NOTE WALL: REDECORATING WITH STORY

Here's how I use sticky notes to generate ideas. I lay out my wall the same way that I talked about in a previous chapter, with a column for each of the acts. I put the five sticky notes (Act 1, Act 2A, Turn, Act 2B, and Act 3) on the wall. As I type this, my office wall is full of sticky notes for different plots I have been working on. There are four novels, a story, and a nonfiction craft book (this one) on the wall. It's a good way to keep track of projects. When I begin the imagining of a novel, I often start with the premise or with the main character. Sometimes, it's one or the other, but for me, it's almost always a premise.

BRAINSTORMING THE PREMISE: WHAT TO PUT ON THE WALL

I write the premise on a sticky note, and I put it right on the wall. Then I brainstorm ideas about the premise. Or if I start with a character, then I brainstorm about the character. I just slap sticky notes on the wall. The initial brainstorming is usually very fast, and my handwriting is usually very bad because my brain is moving faster than my Sharpie. I like to generate the beginnings of a story.

As I mentioned before, we don't use a cork board for this process. It's hard to move things around on a cork board, which tend to be either small or stationary. You have to use stick pins, and you stick yourself. If you want to work on the plot, you have to be in front of the board.

If we were doing a workshop, or if I was consulting one-on-one with you, I could suggest what to write on the stickies. There's something of an art to what to write, which I didn't realize until people tried to brainstorm without having seen the process in person. The best way, I think, to show you what to write is to show you examples of real sticky note plots I've done.

The first example will be from *Soul Enchilada*, my debut novel and also the first novel I used this process with. The second example is from my novel with the working title Jayhawkers, which is still in draft form (and may remain in draft forever). My hope is that using two examples will illustrate the flexibility of the method.

The premise of the *Soul Enchilada* is that a demon repo man is sent to repossess a car from a teenager named Bug. It's not just any car, though. It's a 1957 Cadillac Biarritz. It is a massive chunk of rolling steel and glass, and it has a grill that looks like a monster grinning. That grill is why I chose the make and model.

But I didn't start brainstorming with the premise. I started with the first line, which had popped into my head earlier: "Somebody stole my Cadillac last night." After quickly scribbling that line and slapping it onto the wall, I wrote out a handful of stickies, each one with a short sentence about the premise. Once that was over, I started generating questions about the hero.

EXAMPLE TEXT: SOUL ENCHILADA

I wondered as I looked at the stickies I had placed, what kind of character would say that opening line? I knew it would be teen because I was writing a book for teens, and I knew it would be a girl because the voice in my head sounded like a girl. Then I started to pile crap on them to see how they would react. By crap, I mean complications—twists and turns in their life that make their life more difficult (notice that I only want to make writers' lives easier).

These stickies went on the wall:

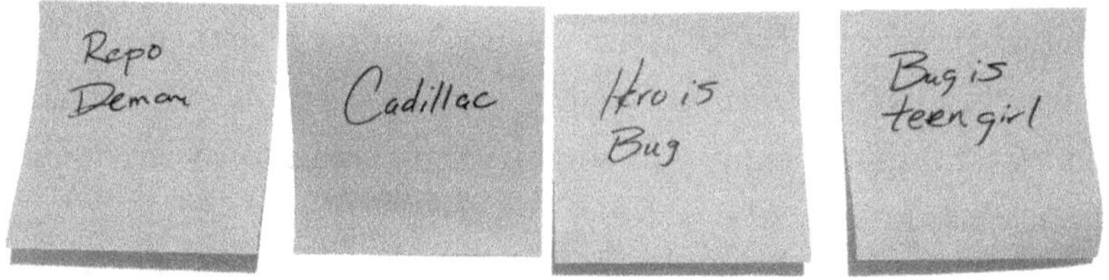

FOUR NOTES THAT BECAME A NOVEL

You don't have to know everything at this stage: I returned to the "taking the car because???" question and many other open questions later. Setting, time, characters, and complications all fell into place. As I brainstormed, ideas came from all different directions—they were about the premise, about Bug, about the grandfather, about the demon, about the car.

I didn't worry about ordering the ideas or even deciding if they were good or not. Every idea that came to be went on the wall. When we are equally open to really cool ideas and really bad ideas, we end up with more stickies overall. Don't edit. Don't reject. Just scribble and stick and ride the wave of creative energy. This is the imaginative part that starts any novel, and the energy is what drives us to write. Remember that drive because we'll have to tap into it later when we need motivation to finish the wall.

That's how *Soul Enchilada* was created over fifteen years ago. To give you a more recent look at the process, let's move on to the second example, *Jayhawkers*. This novel is still in draft form. It started out as an example that I created for a sticky note workshop, but the premise had enough spark that I kept working on it.

Sidenote: I love history, but I try not to write purely historical novels. They don't sell very well, and because of the research required, they take a long time to write. Which is why this novel is still in draft.

EXAMPLE TEXT: JAYHAWKERS

For *Jayhawkers*, I decided on a story set in 1858, as the United States was fighting regional battles over whether or not the country was going to spread slavery out West. The most vicious battles were fought near the Kansas-Missouri border. The territory was called Bleeding Kansas for a reason.

Remember, world-building isn't just part of genre fiction, it's part of every genre. If you set the novel in New York, be aware that everybody thinks they know what New York looks like. Many readers don't, thinking that it's like the set of *Friends*. New York is a vast collection of tiny communities. Ground your reader in one specific community. If you set a novel in Sheboygan, you still have to build the world. How many readers know what Sheboygan is like? Maybe not a ton, but if you get the details of the town wrong, your reader is going to question you, and that is death to the fictive dream.

Anyway, the setting was the first thing I knew (the first sticky was "Kansas 1858"). It was a perfect place for external conflict. But who would feel the conflict? The hero obviously, but who would it be? I scribbled "homestead family" and "youngest son" on stickies and slapped them onto the wall. Homesteaders were often caught in the middle of the battle between proslavery "Bushwhackers" and antislavery "Jayhawkers." Youngest sons often feel like they have something to prove.

On the wall, my character became age 14 (I wrote "Hero is 14") At that time, a fourteen-year-old was on the cusp of manhood, and that would mean that my Hero was changing at the same time the world around them was changing. I liked the synchronicity, which gave me a lot to poke at. My hero was kind, while his brothers were jerks. He was smaller, and at least one of the brothers was big. All that went on stickies. So did his working name: Zeke.

Then I wondered, what is wrong? What does Zeke need? Well, he wants to grow up, to prove himself, and earn his family's trust. How does Zeke lose his family's trust? I don't know, so "How does he lose his family's trust?" goes on the wall. Because I don't know yet, but I need to know that later.

A quick pause: Notice that the notes are a mix of things I know and things that I need to know? This method thrives in the space between the known and unknown, and it is fluid enough to encourage and record that process. Stay fluid during this phase. **Say yes to everything**. After all, it's just a sticky note, and stickies can easily be tossed.

Back to the wall: Zeke was hunting razorbacks with his brothers one day. When the wild boar was in his sights, he didn't shoot. His father was mauled, and now his family thinks he's a coward. Because he froze up, he has the desire to prove himself, but his family won't give him the chance to—or so he thinks (this is his misbelief).

A quick review of the stickies with the things I know:

- The setting? Kansas, 1855. Bleeding Kansas.
- Who's my main character? Zeke.
- His problem? His family doesn't trust him anymore. They think he's a coward.
- His action? He joins John Brown's forces (see below)

Enter John Brown, our maybe villain. Brown was righteous, ethical, and driven to abolish slavery. Brown was on the side of right, but he would kill anybody who opposed his cause. He launched the beginnings of the Civil War by attacking Harper's Ferry in Virginia. Before Harper's Ferry, he and his sons were in Kansas, where they led a guerrilla campaign against proslavery "Bushwhackers."

After meeting Brown, Zeke joined Brown's forces. This decision ends Act 1, so it was the Key Scene where Zeke accepts the Call to Action, and in this case, that action is based on a misbelief about his family. On the wall, I moved to Act 2A and changed the color of the sticky notes I was using. When I first started using this method, I didn't change the colors of sticky notes. I used the basic yellow ones. But after a few plots were under my belt, I realized that using different colors allowed me to see the acts more easily when I glanced at the wall. It also showed how many scenes I moved from one act to another and how the flow of a story could continue even into the later stages of the process.

At the start of Act 2A, Zeke needs to learn how to be a guerrilla soldier, so he starts a training process. On the wall go:

- Brown tells Zeke, "I need great soldiers."
- Zeke says, "I don't know how to do that," but he vows to try.

I know that other (at this point, unknown) good stuff happened, and Brown gave Zeke the honor of becoming a scout. He felt like he had gotten the respect he always wanted. Just like at the end of Act 1, there is a Key Scene at the end of Act 2A. It is the False Victory. Up to this point, Zeke had seen some hardships, but generally, his life with Brown had been pretty easy, and it seemed as if he was going to reach his goal.

Seemed.

Having read about Key Scenes, you can guess what happens next.

As a scout, Zeke discovered a Bushwhackers camp. He led Brown's army there, not knowing what John would do. Zeke thought Brown was a wonderful, Christian man. He saw Brown as a father figure because his own family wouldn't pay attention to him. But it was a shock to Zeke when Brown's army massacred the Bushwhackers. In the aftermath, Zeke recognized one of the dead as a neighbor. Now Zeke has participated in a mass killing, and his whole world turns upside down.

That's the Turn.

It went on the Wall.

When you first start planning the novel, you're probably not going to know the Turn is. Why would you? The Turn is going to be something that destroys what you've created on the wall. You can't destroy what you've created until you have created it. I get chills because now I have a story! That's the physiological reaction I get when a story rings true to me—I get chills, and the hairs on my arm stand up. Weird but true.

To get to this point in the story took me about ten minutes. Ten minutes! This is me trying things on. That's what Sticky Note Plotting does—it lets you quickly try things on to see if they fit. If they don't work, you toss them. Just crumple up the sticky and toss it. If it does work, then you get chills and keep on mining that story strand.

Looking more closely, I can see some good story ideas, but there are lots of gaps, too. The next step is to fill in all the gaps so that I know what the Key Scenes are. By the time I sticky note the end of the story in Act 3, Zeke saves his family homestead and leaves John Brown. He defends his family, and they love him for it. Or hate him. I'm not sure yet. There are lots of holes from the Turn to the ending. Lots of story ideas that need time to develop into strands that I can build. But I know from experience that the villain is going to take over in Act 2B. I just don't know if that's going to be John Brown (the obvious choice) or another character closer to Zeke's age. Filling in the gaps between the known and unknown will give me the answers.

ANOTHER STICKY IN THE WALL

After the initial rush of ideas, I step back and contemplate the wall. I'm looking at individual stickies, but I'm also looking for gaps, at what's missing, or connections. I look for certain key things, like setting, characters, conflict, and stakes. The point is you're going to allow this to be in front of you, going to let the ideas percolate, you're going to allow them to generate, and you're going to work on writing scenes that you think might work or ideas, and along the way, you will start sticking them until you start coming up with enough scenes to flesh out all three acts.

WE AREN'T MAKING STICKY ART

Remember as you're relaxing after a job well done, that there is no inherent value in the sticky notes themselves. The only value is in the process of planning the plot, brainstorming, coming up with all the elements, and being sure the elements are in place before you begin writing the first draft. Every so often, a workshop participant will want to preserve their sticky notes. Three months after a workshop, I'll ask, "How's it going? Have you finished editing the first draft?" They say something like, "I haven't started the novel yet, but I do have this great sticky note wall," and they send me these incredibly complex sticky note walls that look like works of art.

Except they aren't art. Sticky Note Walls are not meant to be art. They are meant to create art.

When writing a novel, we get really excited when we work on that first 50 to 100 pages, but often our excitement kind of fades. If we use the sticky notes to create a plot outline, we can let the anticipation of writing the novel build. By the time we begin writing the novel, we are excited about the whole process, not just the beginning. We also don't get that sudden rush of falling in love with our novel and then falling out of love with it 10,000 words into the first draft. We know what we're getting ourselves into before the heavy lifting starts.

NOT SUITABLE FOR FRAMING

FINISHING THE FIRST STICKY NOTE PLOT WALL

Now comes the hard part. It's the part that will test your patience. Because if you're like, you're desperate to start writing the novel instead of plotting it. But you can't. Not yet. In the writing world, the word marinade is often used to describe the act of letting a story rest. You could also use a sourdough metaphor and say that the story needs time to rise. It's true. Just like the dough needs time for those tiny bubbles to form in the dough, your Sticky Note Plot needs time for deeper connections to form in your writer's brain. Your subconscious brain needs time to bubble up, and if you give it time to breathe, if definitely will.

You see, the initial flurry of building the Sticky Note Wall is all about speed. Getting ideas on the wall as soon as they form so that you can capture everything. At first, all ideas are equal. As the story develops and as you slow down to contemplate possibilities, the process slows. Some ideas become more valuable than others. Indeed, some of those early ideas become irrelevant, and you remove them from the Wall. At some point, the generation of ideas will end, and you will be staring at a vibrant but incomplete story. You may be tempted to call it good enough and try to move on to the next step in the Sticky Note process.

Don't do it.

Step away from the Wall. Go about your life. But carry a sticky note pad and Sharpie as you go about your life. If an idea strikes you while you're doing chores, commuting to work, doing the garden, or taking a run, jot it down. If you dream about the word you've created, write down your dream. Keep doing this for a few days.

Then, go back to the Sticky Note Wall. Count the number of relevant stickies. If you have less than 80 stickies, you're not ready yet. Let the story marinate some more. If you have 80100, you're in good shape and can check your wall for these items:

- Are there an equal number of stickies in each Act? With four columns on the Wall, that's 2025. If not, fill them out.
- Are the Key Scenes evident in each Act? Point to them. Literally put your finger on the sticky and state the events of each Key Scene.
- Is there a definitive Turn in the middle? How is the hero devastated? How is the course of the story forever changed? What is the point of no return?
- Does Act 2B have a clear purpose? Make sure it has the same number of stickies as the other Acts. Don't be tempted to skip ahead, thinking, oh I'll fill out in the written draft. That almost never happens.

- Does Act 3 show the hero's change? Is the final battle with the villain satisfying?
- Does the final scene show that the story has come full circle? Has the world itself changed?

If you can't answer the questions or if the Turn just isn't making itself known, then take more time to marinade. You will get there, no matter how long it takes.

For the purposes of the process, let's assume that you've gone through the checklist and fixed all that needs fixing. You're ready for the next step, which leads to creating a first draft using sticky notes. If I were in your shoes, I'd be champing at the bit to get something on paper, so I'm guessing that you are too.

Ready?

ACTIVITIES
DIGGING DEEPER

The two examples I shared, *Soul Enchilada* and *Jayhawkers*, look very similar on a Sticky Note Wall. They have roughly the same number of stickies, and they both have all the Key Scenes. The process of getting those stickies in place, however, was very different.

Before planning *Soul Enchilada*, I had used components of the process on other novels. It was during the fairly long, winding, and random ordeal of figuring out how to plot a "loud" book that publishers would notice that the Sticky Note process gel led for me. It took a long time to put all those stickies in order and then even longer to figure out how to turn them into a manuscript. With *Jayhawkers*, the process was much faster because I've had lots of practice, having plotted literally dozens of novels with students and writer friends since *Soul Enchilada*.

When you're learning a new process, it takes time to learn the process, so the outcome may take longer than you expect.

The length of time to do a Sticky Note Plot is not predictive of how long it will take to write the planned novel. *Soul Enchilada* took about four months to draft. *Jayhawkers* is still unfinished.

EXERCISE 1

Since you're using this book to learn a process, it makes sense to practice the process. Grab a copy of a favorite novel. Using the SNP method, create a Sticky Note Wall. Write a sticky for every Key Scene, as well as important details of the story. When you finish, a casual observer, someone who has not read the book, should be able to track the story using only the stickies.

STICKY NOTE CHECKLIST: THE STICKY NOTE PLOT

- A premise, which is a short statement of the novel's setup, can come from anywhere, and it can initially get the creative juices flowing. That doesn't mean that it has enough juice to sustain a novel.
- In the first burst of creative energy, write down everything you can think about the story. It doesn't matter what order you write stuff down.
- The strength of the Sticky Note Plot process is its flexibility. You can start at any point and go in any direction. There will be time later to put everything into order.
- Does the book end with the hero and the world changed?

CHAPTER 6
THE BEAT SHEET

THE STEP AFTER FINISHING A STICKY NOTE PLOT is creating a beat sheet. Now that I've explained how to create a sticky note plot, I'm going to explain how I use Microsoft Word, Scrivener, and a Sticky Note template to create a novel beat sheet. Then I'll tell you how I create a first draft from the beat sheet. It's an easy process, but there are lots of steps, so stick with me.

The first thing you need to know: Writing a first draft from a Sticky Note beat sheet is crazy fast. It can be a wild ride, so hang on.

CREATING A BEAT SHEET: THE MAP TO BUILDING A FIRST DRAFT

For the next step, I'm assuming that you have finished the Sticky Note Plot (seriously, if you're just skipping ahead, go back and finish the Wall). The formerly blank wall is loaded with little sticky notes. They are arranged in colors. There are 80 to 100 of them. There is a combination of specific scenes, character development, scenery, plot points, or backstory/flashbacks. All the Key Scenes are there. The acts are fairly proportional. You probably have some scenes that are not quite there. Others that are very well fleshed out. There is a Turn. It may not be perfect, but at least it does the basic purpose of the story, and you have an ending. So what do you do with all these sticky notes? Well, you could leave them on the wall for months at a time, languishing and waiting for someone to love them.

Or you could collect them and create what we call a beat sheet.

The concept of a beat sheet comes from screenwriting. A beat sheet is just a list of scenes that are important to the story. A beat is the smallest unit of a story, smaller than an act or even a scene. We will get these story beats from the sticky notes. Which means that we are going to remove the stickies from the wall, starting from the end of Act 3. Make a stack of the stickies, with the end of Act 3 on the bottom and the beginning of Act 1 on the top.

This is what I do: I stack up the 80 to 100 sticky notes and put the stack next to the computer. I open a Word doc and type each note in the document. Each sticky note is a single line on the document. After the note is typed in, I hit return and go to the next note. When I am finished typing in all the notes, the Word doc becomes my beat sheet, which is just a sequence of story events. Next, I review each line for information that doesn't fit—because I said "yes" to every-thing during the sticky note process, I end up with a few irrelevant storylines, details, or characters. I delete anything that no longer fits. But I will leave in details or descriptions that are important to the story so far. Now I'm ready for the next step, getting the document ready for writing. At this point, you can choose to use two different types of software to use for creating a first draft. If you only use Word (or another word processor) for writing, then you will, as I show below, use the beat sheet for drafting the novel. If you use a story creation app such as Scrivener, then I will show you how to import the beat into the app and how to expand it into a first draft.

USING WORD TO EXPAND THE BEAT SHEET INTO A FIRST DRAFT

Word (substitute your favorite word processor here) is a tried-and-true tool for writing a novel. It has most of the basic tools necessary to hammer out a first draft. But opening a blank doc can be kind of intimidating, so we're going to use the beat sheet to create a workflow for the first draft. Here's how:

- Open the beat sheet document. Next, open Word's "advanced find and replace" function. In the search box type in a period followed by pilcrow, the symbol for paragraph returns. (.¶). Use the replace function to replace the period and pilcrow with a manual page break (^m).
- Voila! Now each line of the beat sheet is on a separate page. Starting with the first line of the first page, start fleshing out the details of the scene. I usually head each new page—which will be a scene once you're done—with the following:
- Place:
- Time:
- Weather:
- Characters in the scene:
- Events of the scene:
- Scene goal (more on that later)

Then I write a short intro paragraph that either summarizes the action or if they are clear in my mind, the actions themselves. Bits of dialogue may pop into my mind. If so, I write them down. If actions related to the dialogue seem necessary, I'll type those out, too. Maybe next, some bits of interior monologue come to me. I'll write those down too, sometimes in context to the dialogue and sometimes, related to nothing else.

Since I'm on a roll, other bits of information come out of the blue. Maybe details about the hero and other characters. Maybe some backstory. Maybe some secrets— secrets!—that have been hidden.

Maybe more actions, these being specific to the scene.

Does the process of generating ideas feel familiar? That's because this is the exact same process of using sticky notes to make a wall. It's about building on an idea, filling in blanks, and letting ideas come to you in any order. That's why we don't just start scenes in the sequential, concrete order of "this happens, then this, then that." Your story is not ready yet to be locked into that type of thinking. You're still using the Sticky Note plot method to create scenes. You're just not using the stickies to do it now.

Let's assume that you've spent a while on that first scene. You've generated a page or two of action, dialogue, monologue, backstory, and maybe some random ideas. What's next? Move on to the next scene. Fill out the data about place, time, weather, etc. Do the summary. Now repeat the process from the first scene. Take the story as far as you can. When you run out of steam, move on to the next scene. But wait! An idea about Scene 1 has popped into your head. Great! Scroll back up to that scene and type the idea in. That's the advantage of drafting this way—since it's still a living document, you can bounce around all you want.

That's it. You keep fleshing out each scene until every scene has been expanded. Lather, rinse, repeat. Some scenes will be longer than others. That's expected. Personally, I write chunks of prose that may or may not be connected. Others write more of a traditional draft. Others still write the minimum number of words. It's your choice. How long will this part of the process take? I have no idea! Every writer works at a different pace. Every book is different. The key is to stick with it. Make sure that every scene is expanded before you move on to the next step in the Sticky Note Plot Process.

USING SCRIVENER TO EXPAND THE BEAT SHEET INTO A FIRST DRAFT

This section is for writers who use Scrivener to draft novels. If you are happy using Word and aren't interested in any other app, then you can skip this section, but if you're curious about what Scrivener can do, then I invite you to read this part. I love Scrivener. It is my favorite tool for writing. I've created several novels on it. I've also written research papers, essays, short stories, graphic novels, blog posts, and the very book that you're now reading. Scrivener has a few features in it that make it perfect for working on novels. It has an import and split function that allows you to import a Word document and automatically split the document into separate chapters.

To do that, I open the beat sheet and then choose Word's search function. I do a search for a period followed by pilcrow, the symbol for paragraph returns. (.¶). Then I use the replace function to replace the period and pilcrow with a dollar sign ($).

So I open Scrivener. I choose a template that I created specifically for Sticky Note novels. I label the new file with the working title of the rough draft. Here's where the magic happens.

In Scrivener, I select the **File>Import** feature and then choose Import and Split. Then once the dialogue box opens up, I open the file, and Scrivener automatically looks for the dollar sign $ character I put in and splits each of the lines from the beat sheet into a different scene.

This import creates a single document of 80 to 100 scenes that can be fleshed out. Since each line forms the first line of a scene, I start at the top and work my way through the beat sheet, expanding each of those beats. I label the time, place, and situation for each scene.

This is not literary prose. This is not narrative that the reader will ever read. This is information for me, the author, so that I can create a rudimentary sequence of events for the novel. If I don't know the time and place, I type a question mark so that I can come back to it later. For each of the scenes, I block out the basic action. This document looks a lot like a screenplay, but you could always write your draft so that it looks like a conventional draft. It's your decision.

BLOCKING OUT THE ACTION: HOW THE CHARACTERS MOVE

Now I begin to block out the action. Unlike the time, date, and place stamp, what I write now may be words that the reader will later read. So I tend to write in a more narrative form. However, my narrative still looks more like a screenplay than a novel, which is just my personal preference.

Why? Because screenplays take place in the now. The action is visible and therefore, filmable. Why does it matter if a novel is filmable? Because filmable means the characters are active, and active characters are engaging characters. I have to do it this way because of my natural inclination to write "quiet" scenes. Unlike novels where you can get into the character's head, a screenplay won't allow you to show the character's thoughts. When getting into a character's head, many of us writers forget about moving the character around. So we end up with a bunch of static pages with no action at all. If action can't be shown, then it doesn't belong in the beat sheet. We will do thoughts and feelings in a later pass.

I block out the action so that I know what the character does. For example, the beats are the hero goes to the store, buys a candy bar, then walks out into the street where they see a robbery/car chase/alien/proposal/ghost. In the middle of blocking, I may write rudimentary dialogue. Why? It's important to understand how the characters feel, how they talk, how they interact with the world, and how they might express themselves.

I type my way through the beat sheet, blocking out the action and expanding the beats of the story so that the plot begins to take form. We want not only to see what the characters are doing, but also to see how they interact with one another and their world. I block out all the scenes until I reach the end of the beat sheet.

WORD AND SCRIVENER USERS UNITE

Whether you used Word or Scrivener to flesh out the beat sheet, the end product is the same: You now have a finished (and very loose) first draft. By "finished," I mean that you have written scenes for all of the major events of the story, including the ending. It's very important to reach the ending because the way that the story ends will change how it's supposed to begin.

Once you finish this process, there's no need for the sticky notes you used to build the first wall. Throw them away. I really mean that. Throw them all away. You've already transcribed them in the first draft, and if you keep them around, you may be tempted to reuse them. Don't. We will be returning to using sticky notes again, and you'll want to start fresh with a new wall. Okay, you now have a first draft. What's next? It's time for the first revision pass. I recommend doing revisions in passes. With each pass, you are looking for specific elements of the story, such as action, dialogue, characterization, etc. I've found it easier to do multiple passes, rather than slogging through revision one scene at a time, trying to fix everything in the scene all at once.

Note: you are still not writing the novel in the usual sense of the word. You're expanding the Sticky Notes beats into larger scenes. I start the first revision pass at the top with the first scene. There, I expand the action and add more dialogue. At the top of the scene, I nail down the placeholders for the time, date, and setting. If I know what the scene goal is (more on that later), I write it below the setting. If I can, I create the lede, the information that the reader needs to understand the context of the scene.

Setting is very important to each scene. If we establish setting now, we don't have to do it later. It's really difficult to backfill setting and worldbuilding.

Blocking—the physical movements of a character—isn't just about going to the store, buying a candy bar, and walking outside to witness a kidnapping. It's about the little actions that bring the character to life. This is where we build stakes and conflict.

When writing dialogue, it helps to know what the agenda is for the character. When they talk, what do they want? What are they willing to do to get it? What is their purpose here and how much truth are they going to reveal? All characters lie. They may lie directly or indirectly or by omission, but they leave out information that other characters need. This creates conflict and complications, which is a very good way to introduce characters.

Most novels can handle about a dozen active characters who interact with each other. Once you go beyond that number, the reader can become confused, and the story often will become convoluted. So if you're writing a straightforward, less than 100,000-word novel, it's helpful to limit yourself to a dozen characters who are fully formed and interactive.

Once you break down 80 to 100 scenes, you might notice that some of them are very well formed. That's because your brain was pinging, you were deep in the fictive dream, and the ideas were flowing. Some of the scenes, though, are still bare bones. They are just a placeholder until something better comes along. You're not quite sure what happens next, and that's okay. Next, look at each Act and identify the Key Scenes. Make sure that you can state (by writing it at the top of the scene) a summary of the Key Scene's action, the scene question, and the hero's scene goal.

The first revision pass is a great time to begin working on the Turn. Find it. Mark it as the Turn. Make sure that it is still in the middle of the story. Turns tend to drift later in the story timeline during the creation of the first draft, often slipping past the midpoint and sometimes, all the way to the three quarters point. Experience has taught me that writers have the firmest grip on Act 1. They know the hero. They know the premise. The Call to Action may be a little shaky, but it's enough to launch the journey of Act 2A.

The journey starts smoothly, mostly because of the Hero's Montage and the budding relationships, but after the writer reaches the Turn, the action tends to meander. Characters stop developing. The scenes get shorter. Some scenes are still just a summary of the action. Act 2B becomes maybe 1/3rd or 1/4th the size of Act 1. With nothing much going on, the writer skips to Act 3. They hurry to reach the Dark Night of the Soul, followed by a mad dash to reach the final, climactic battle and the resolution to the story. Thus, Act 3, while not as thin as Act 2B, is a skeleton frame with two or three fleshed-out scenes.

And that's okay for a first draft.

Rome wasn't built in a day, and the novel won't be complete after a first draft. Or a second. Maybe even a third. With the Sticky Note Plot process, we keep filling in the gaps, fleshing out the scenes, and building the story piece by piece.

SCENE QUESTIONS, CHARACTER GOALS, AND KICKERS

Once the first revision pass is finished and I am satisfied that the big story elements are in place, I return to the first scene in the draft. This time when I read the scene, I write a one or two-sentence summary of the action on a sticky note. I put the sticky note on my new wall (remember that I told you to throw away the old stickies). I also make sure that each scene has a scene question, and I write the scene question—which is the must-be-answered question in the reader's mind when they begin reading the scene on a sticky note. It goes on the wall. Next, I write character goals—the thing the character wants to achieve on a sticky. Simultaneously, I type the scene questions and character goals from the new wall into my Spreadsheet of Doom, which is a spreadsheet that contains almost every element for writing scenes, and it will force me to confront the weaknesses in the novel.

It is common for scene questions and goals to change during the revision process. It doesn't matter if the questions and goals change. Like the rest of the Sticky Note process, they're not written in stone. They're just temporary pins for ideas—holding places in your brain—to give you something to work from. The important thing for now is that you understand that scene questions need to be there.

While doing the summary and writing down the scene questions, also start looking for kickers. Kickers are the endings of scenes that compel the reader forward. They're the hook that sets the scene question in the reader's mind as a precursor before the next scene or chapter. You don't have to have great kickers yet, but it helps to identify potential lines, images, dialogue, or questions that you can build on later.

SCENE ORDER

The last thing to consider during this phase is the sequence of the scenes. Are things happening in the right order? Does this scene in Act 1 actually need to be in Act 2A? Does the argument between the hero and their best friend work better in Act 2B? If you draft in a word processor like Microsoft Word, it's difficult and confusing to reorder scenes.

When I used to revise in Word, I would find myself scrolling back and forth to find the information that I needed. Did this event where my character bought the Hershey bar the first time occur in Chapter 2 or Chapter 3? When they go to the store to buy another one, does that occur in Chapter 14 or Chapter 15?

Madness!

After I switched drafting in Scrivener, this major headache went away (mostly). Because of the way it's structured, Scrivener allows the user to move between those scenes simply by clicking on the name of the scene on the lefthand binder bar. I can move quickly and efficiently through the text, bouncing from one scene to the next. If I want to reorder a scene, I simply click and drag it to its new spot in the scene order. Need to cut a scene out completely? Just click on the scene in the Binder and hit delete. Voila! It goes into the trash. With Scrivener, nothing is deleted forever. It just drops it into the trash at the bottom so you can come back and recover it later, but it gets it off your plate and out of your mind.

So that ends what we're doing with the beat sheet section. Now we export the draft document into Word and begin the true first draft revision, which begins with....the Sticky Notes Process, Phase Two!

ACTIVITIES
DIGGING DEEPER

The discovery of the beat sheet idea changed how I wrote first drafts. Previously, I had opened a blank Word document and started typing what I imagined was the opening scene of the novel. It was a very slow process. I carefully weighed and measured every word. Inevitably, I would throw away all of those precious words during revision, realizing that the story hadn't begun in that place at all. It's very discouraging to toss good writing. I was loath to do it, which made me less likely to do substantial revisions. Maybe you do that too. Maybe the beat sheet will change how you write first drafts, too.

- Scenes written from a beat sheet will be far looser, and the writing will be pedestrian.
- Scenes are initially just blocking and dialogue.
- You will probably be more willing to toss scenes that don't work since the time commitment to write them is minimal.
- Scenes can be written out of order.

- The scenes themselves can be written piecemeal and in no given sequence. You aren't forced to write sequentially.

EXERCISE 1

I will often default to first-person, present tense when hammering out the beat sheet, which is a problem later if I change the narrative to say, third-person past. It's worth considering POV and verb tense before fleshing out the beat sheet. Although it's entirely possible to change both POV and verb tense later, it's just a time-consuming pain in the butt, which is a pain we always want to avoid. For this exercise, decide which POV and verb tense you want to use. Go through your manuscript and change all POV and verbs to match your choice.

EXERCISE 2

Using Scrivener's Import and Split function, import the Word doc. Pick a scene that looks interesting and start expanding it. Block out the character action. Write some dialogue. Throw in a couple of setting details. Sprinkle in some interior thoughts and/or feelings. Maybe write a few more lines of dialogue. Move stuff around. Keep piling in the verbal fill dirt.

EXERCISE 3

Once you've filled in one scene, pick the next scene and repeat the process. Block the action. Write the dialogue. Sprinkle in setting. Lather. Rinse. Repeat.

STICKY NOTE CHECKLIST: THE BEAT SHEET

- The primary purpose of a beat sheet is to create a list of scenes to be fleshed out.
- Scrivener is the best writing software I've found because it allows me to reorder scenes easily.
- Blocking (the characters' physical movements) is the little actions that form the character's implied personality.
- Blocking is also where we build stakes and conflict.
- Expanding the beat sheet also allows us to experiment with dialogue for all characters.
- Strong characters have an agenda. When writing dialogue, it helps to know what the character's agenda is.
- If an idea for a new scene pops into your brain, seize the moment and write it on a sticky. Put it on the wall! The Sticky Note process doesn't stop!

CHAPTER 7
STICKY NOTES PHASE TWO

WHEN WE BEGIN A FIRST DRAFT, we're bursting with the thrill of inspiration, but the thrill can fade as we slog through the rest of the draft. We get really excited working on the first 50100 pages, and then reality sets in. Writing a novel is a ton of work, and it's easy to get lost on the plot and lose steam.

Ugh.

By using the sticky notes, by creating a plot outline, we can prolong the enjoyment of writing a novel: As we build the story on the wall, our excitement builds. Because we know what's coming down the road story-wise, we don't ever feel lost or overwhelmed just because the initial rush of creation is over.

It's time to make a new rush! Let's start plotting again!

BRAINSTORMING PHASE TWO

After finishing a first draft, I grab a new stack of sticky notes. For each scene (not chapter), I write a one-sentence summary of the scene and put it on the wall. I do this for every scene. When I finish, I see the old same pattern from plotting out the first draft (and also when I'm story coaching a writer who has finished their first draft): A lopsided sticky note plot.

I bet that the revised Sticky Note Plot will be lopsided too. Like most people, you have probably written a very good Act 1. You have a pretty good Act 2A. You have a moderately effective Turn. You've written a pretty decent Act 3, which is the ending, and almost everybody works on their ending.

But wait, what's this? An anemic 2B, smack dab in the second part of the second act. Uh-oh. Houston, we have a problem. Since the first draft is about discovering the story of the hero, Act 2B is where the hero takes a backseat to other characters, and chances are, the other characters haven't been developed yet. Because of this, first drafts tend to be one-dimensional.

How do you fix it? With a thing called a B-Story.

THE B-STORY: THE SWISS ARMY KNIFE OF PLOT TOOLS

The **B-Story** is the story that complements the main story. It helps the writer carry the action through Act 2B, as it adds an extra layer of complication to the story. Many people use the term subplot instead of B-Story. Novels certainly can have lots of subplots, but the B-Story is a lot more robust than a subplot because it acts as a mirror to the main plot.

To illustrate the concept of a B-Story, I'll use one of the classics of the 1990s, Pixar's *Toy Story*. *Toy Story* is a movie, not a novel, but its B-Story is an excellent example. With a viewing time of 90 minutes, it's easy to watch. So go watch *Toy Story,* even if you've seen it before, and then come back for the explication of the B-Story.

Pretend that we've done a Sticky Note Plot together, including the Key Scenes. Because he is the de facto POV character, Woody's story is the A-story. So we put Woody's story on top, so to speak because it is the main narrative. Buzz, then, gets the B-Story, and we mix the stickies about his narrative through line in with Woody's story. It's easy to lose the B-Story on the Sticky Note Wall, so to track the progression of a B-Story, I connect the sticky notes by taping a piece of red string to every note that includes Buzz's B-Story. The string can get heavy enough to pull the stickies down, so make sure that the stickies are firmly attached to the wall. Putting the string up shows Buzz's character arc more visually. Remember, the first purpose of the Sticky Note Plot is to visualize the story so that you can look at the big picture. Look for symmetry. Look for progression. Look for character arcs.

ACTING ON A MISBELIEF: WHY CHARACTERS DO THE WRONG THING FOR THE RIGHT REASONS

Our first B-Story sticky note shows Buzz entering and physically knocking Woody aside. Next, the red string connects to where Buzz is flying and taking over the room as Woody gets more jealous. In the next scene, Buzz is knocked out of the window. Then Buzz hitchhikes in the family van. On the way to Pizza Planet, Buzz fights with Woody in the back seat. After the altercation, Buzz decides to work with Woody, but he's still delusional in his misbelief: He thinks that they're in a space station, not a pizza place. Because of Buzz's misbelief, his actions lead him to a claw machine full of LGMs (Little Green Men), where at the Turn, he and Woody are captured by Syd, Andy's sadistic neighbor. Syd takes Buzz and Woody to his house, and they encounter the scary toys that Syd has altered. At this point, Buzz and Woody split up. The next few scenes belong to Woody, so on the Sticky Note Wall, our red string skips those scenes. Buzz essentially disappears from the story.

We run the red string to the scene where Buzz reappears. As he cases the house looking for Commander Zorg (the villain from Buzz's "reality"), he sees himself (and Zorg) on a TV commercial. In an epiphanic moment, Buzz realizes that he is indeed a toy, but he tries one more time to prove that he can fly. His attempt fails miserably, and he tumbles down a stairwell, his arm detached.

Although he is rescued by Syd's kid sister, Buzz goes into a deep, dark depression, getting drunk on Darjeeling tea. He remains there, refusing Woody's help, until (and our red string skips scenes) the misfit toys reattach Buzz's arm, which snaps him out of his funk. However, both Buzz and Woody are recaptured by Syd, who takes to the backyard, where he tapes a real rocket to Buzz. In true heroic fashion, Buzz grabs Woody, and they light the rocket. In this moment of crisis, Buzz finally overcomes his misbelief. He acts to save Woody and himself by using the very abilities that make him a great Space Ranger. He accepts his true identity while staying true to himself.

Buzz flies!

But he understands that he's just "falling with style" because he can't really fly. He's a toy. But he's also the B-Story in *Toy Story*. Although Buzz's growth has a direct effect on the main character, Woody has his own character arc. Where does that character arc happen for the most part?

In Act 2B.

Notice that Buzz and Woody are mostly separate during Act 2B. It's okay, and maybe even preferable to let the hero take a step back in 2B while another character steps into the limelight. The novel doesn't have to be all hero all the time. Woody doesn't do much for the rest of 2B, yet in Act 3, he takes over this story again with this character arc, which goes all the way down to the Dark Night of the Soul. In fact, Woody gets his wish to be an action hero when he rescues Buzz. He also gets to scare the crap out of a mean kid, and who wouldn't love that? Finally, he has an epiphany as Buzz is flying. In this way, both character arcs come together at the same moment.

FINDING SYMMETRY: CONNECTING PIECES OF THE STORY

It's difficult to get that kind of symmetry but don't let it stop you from trying. Look for symmetry. Look for connections. Look for chances to echo themes, ideas, or phrases. In Toy Story, both Woody and Buzz use the phrase "falling with style." Even though they mean different things when they say it, the phrase unites them and unites their story arcs. To sum up Sticky Note Plot string theory: It's a technique of using a piece of red string to connect the character's arcs. Do this with every B-Story. Use a different color to mark each B-Story. Toy Story has multiple B-Stories (follow the Woody/Bo-Peep story for a great example), and they all have some kind of arc. Try to line up the strings so that they intersect or complement one other. If you can make all the strings converge in Act 3, the novel will have a satisfying ending.

Just to warn you: With all that string, your Sticky Note Wall may end up looking like a work of an overzealous conspiracy theorist. Don't worry. If you're bothered by the mess, you don't have to keep all the strings up. You can take a picture of the wall, then remove the strings. Again, it's a good idea to use sticky notes with stronger glue and if possible, to use chart paper underneath.

You probably can't make all of the B-stories work in a first draft. I'm not sure you can do it in a second or third. But if you keep working on it, keep plotting, keep putting the stickies up there and moving things around, you will eventually get to infinity and beyond.

ACTIVITIES
DIGGING DEEPER

The B-Story fixes an underdeveloped Act 2B. The easiest part of writing a novel is getting the original spark of the premise on the page. The hardest part of writing a novel is bridging the sagging gap between the midpoint Turn to the ending. Remember when I wrote that a good Turn can fix the muddle of the middle? Shifting focus to a B-Story after the Turn will keep the story feeling robust. Giving a secondary character the spotlight will make the fix so much easier.

- The middle is usually a muddle because the A-story isn't complex enough to carry the action to the ending. The B-Story adds that complexity, whether the B-Story shines on a buddy or a bad guy.
- Good bad guys are crucial to the story and to the hero's development. Refusing to include one because you don't like villains is like removing the fourth leg from a chair: It gets really hard to balance things out.

EXERCISE 1

Try the B-Story method on a Sticky Note Wall you've done. Either on another author's novel, your own back burner novel, or a work in progress. Note where the B-Story takes over and where it disappears.

EXERCISE 2

Use different colors of string for each story and track 23 B-stories on your Sticky Note Wall. Do all of the strings reach the end of the novel? Are there any strings that disappear mid-story? Can you think of a way for all the B-stories to come together in a single scene in Act 3?

STICKY NOTE CHECKLIST: STICKY NOTES PHASE 2

- Most first drafts are visually lopsided.
- Like a graphic organizer, looking at the plot-in-progress with stickies and string lets us see where the first draft's structure is weak. We know at a glance what needs fixed.
- The B-Story is the story that complements the main story. It helps the writer carry the action through Act 2B.
- Novels can have lots of subplots, but the B-Story is a lot more robust than a subplot because it acts as a mirror to the main plot.

CHAPTER 8
SCENE STRUCTURE

CCORDING TO THE STICKY NOTE PLOT METHOD, most scenes in a novel (I'd like to say all scenes, but I'll restrain myself) are made of three components: **Exposition**, **Precursors**, and **Action & Aftermath**.

EXPOSITION: SALTING FOR FICTIVE FLAVOR

Exposition is the presentation and/or explanation of information in a story. It is used to form connective tissue for scenes, and like most connective tissues, it is used sparingly and only when needed. Types of exposition are:

- Backstory (things that happened in the story world before the novel began)). See earlier references to Carl Hiaasen's ability to integrate backstory into the narrative without slowing the pace.
- Scenery Description (descriptions of the setting. Keep it short and try to include only the setting details that are important in that particular scene)

- Character Description (descriptions of the characters. Keep it short and try to include only the details that are important in that particular scene. Also, characters are more than their eye color and hair, so describe the body and the clothes.)
- Prior Story Events (what has happened since the last chapter ended)
- Transitions in Space and Time ("in the hours since Tam lost his front teeth, he had walked all the way home, passing three dentist offices along the way"). If these occur at the beginning of a scene, I call them ledes.
- When we're revising based on the Sticky Note Plot method, we write down all of the elements and put them on the way. That's a lot of stickies for each scene, so it's okay to stack those stickies on the wall. They will use up a lot less real estate.

PRECURSORS: THE INVISIBLE INGREDIENTS

Precursors are intangible elements that exist before the scene begins, set in place by previous scenes. Before the reader begins reading the scene, certain elements need to be in place. In the Sticky Note Plot method, the precursors are **Scene Question/Answer**, **Stakes**, and **Desire Line**. We write those on stickies, too, and as with Precursors, it's okay to stack them on the wall.

ACTION & AFTERMATH: THE CORE BUILDING BLOCKS OF A SCENE

Action & Aftermath are a coupled, circular sequence used to advance the action of a story. Actions drive a story forward as the character attempts to achieve a goal. Aftermath lets the character react, take stock of the situation, and choose the next course of action. These actions tend to be too complex to describe on a single sticky, so we use multiple stickies to describe them. Don't stack these stickies on the wall: it's important that you can see all the action at a glance, so put them up one at a time in order of occurrence.

When I began teaching scene structure, I relied on a theory found in *Techniques of the Selling Writer* by Dwight Swain (1965). In his book, Swain defined a scene as a "unit of conflict, an account of an effort to attain a goal despite opposition." Swain defined a sequel as a transition that translates a failure into a goal, telescopes reality, and controls pace.

One of the frustrating things about teaching Swain's scene structure to my writing students was his embedded use of the word scene. Swain uses the word scene to describe a unit of story action. Scene is also used to describe a component of a scene. It's seldom a good idea to name a component of a thing the same name as the thing (it's like saying one of the ingredients of a cake is cake).

So while the term "Scene & Sequel" has been around for decades, the "thing defined by the same thing" definition makes it a confusing term. So instead, I prefer to use **Action & Aftermath**, which makes the relationship more clear.

To review: Scenes are made up of Exposition, Precursors, and Action & Aftermath, and they all go on the wall. Got it? Now I'm going to tell you what's in a scene and how to build one.

SCENE STRUCTURE: SCENE EXPOSITION ELEMENTS

The most basic parts of a scene are the exposition elements. While the quantity of each element varies from scene to scene, they need to be present in every scene, at least minimally. Exposition elements are the mechanics of the scene, the combination of elements that the reader can see written on the page. They are the elements of the physical structure of the scene.

- **Setting**: This is the time and place of the action. Scenes may have multiple settings. Try to establish the setting in the first or second paragraph of a new scene. Don't stop the action for an info/description dump. Often a sentence or a single phrase is enough if the setting is familiar to the reader.
- **POV Character**: This is important for multiple 3rd POVs or for omniscient POV. It also shows if POV was switched during the scene. Generally, it's easier to stay in one POV per scene.
- **Lede**: The lede is the first sentence that shows the gist of the scene. It is often the first sentence of the scene. A lede can also be a "delayed lede," which comes after a more interesting hook. I borrowed this term from journalism, where it means the most important aspect of the story. In my use, the lede is the important information that the reader needs to understand what's happening in the scene.
- **Kicker**: A kicker is the last line of a scene that figuratively kicks the reader into the next scene. Kickers come in all flavors: cliffhangers, dramatic questions, character realizations, plot twists, or hints that there are darker forces at work. Any flavor will do, as long as it's not repetitive and as long as it sets up the scene question for the next scene.
- **Backstory**: This is background information the reader needs to understand the events and emotion of the scene. Backstory is best when delivered in the smallest dose possible as close to when the reader needs it. If written in the form of a flashback, it works more sublimely if the flashback is triggered by a memory or physical action.

SCENE STRUCTURE: PRECURSORS

The first parts of a scene are what I call **Precursors**. A precursor is an object or action that precedes an action or event. In science, a precursor is an essential compound that must be in place before a chemical reaction that produces a different compound can occur. In fiction, I define a precursor as a story element that must be in place before a scene begins. Precursors are not always tangible. Sometimes, they are just ideas, making them tricky to nail down.

SCENE QUESTION/ANSWER

The essential, nonnegotiable elements that every scene must have a **scene question** and the answer that follows it). Without the scene question, there is no reason for the scene to exist in the story. It's easier if the scene question is introduced (or restated) at the end of the previous scene (see note on kickers). There are several possible answers to a scene question: yes, no, yes but, yes and, no but, and no and.

If the answer to the scene question is just plain "yes," it's time to change the scene question because a simple yes minimizes conflict, complications, stakes, and other things that make the scene worth reading. The scene question always goes on the sticky wall, on one sticky. Put it in a prominent place on the wall and read it each time you work on scene. You need to have the question in mind because it governs the action of the scene.

STAKES

Stakes are something that can be won or lost. The higher the stakes, the more the character is risking, and with risk comes reward. Readers love stakes because they are cheering for the hero to succeed. When we write a scene, we always ask: What is at stake for my characters in the scene? Stakes can be both internal and external. External stakes are often what's at stake for the character(s) physically, while internal stakes are often what's at stake for the character(s) emotionally.

Here's where you can do more brainstorming about the scene. Quickly jot down a list of stakes for the hero and the other characters during this scene. Stack them on the wall if you need to. Keep coming back to the stakes, even if you have moved on to other scenes. If a new stake comes to you, put it on the wall. Eventually, your subconscious mind will find the perfect stakes for you.

DESIRE LINE

Every hero has a **desire line**. It's the equivalent of the plot line for the story, and it weaves through every scene, changing based on the events of the scene. What does the character desire? Yearn for? Have to have? What are they willing to give up for it? How does the desire change as the story progresses? That's the desire line. Write the desire line on a sticky and put it on the wall.

SCENE STRUCTURE: PARTS OF ACTION & AFTERMATH—ACTION

This is the **action** and events of the scene, which include the external physical movements of the characters but can also include environmental events (like a landslide or a car accident or meatballs falling from the sky).

Action can happen anywhere in a scene, and it isn't just a big physical activity. It can be as simple as placing a saltshaker on a table. In the Sticky Note method, the parts of a scene are **Goal**, **Conflict**, and **Failure**. If you're feeling a little lost in the weeds by my list of craft terms, it's okay to just read this chapter and wait to apply it later. The terms are necessary to describe parts of the scene, and as you use them on the Sticky Note Wall and with the Spreadsheet of Doom, they will become more familiar.

GOAL

A **goal** is the desired result of a character's actions. The hero's scene goal is specific and obvious to the reader. It is connected to the Scene Q&A: the character goal leads to the answer to the scene question. In a discussion of scene structure in his craft book *Scene and Structure* (1999), Jack Bickham doesn't separate the scene question from the scene goal, and they are often the exact same thing. There are some scenes, however, where the scene question is not answered by the POV character's goal, so the question and the goal have to be stated separately.

CONFLICT

Conflict is essential to a story. Without it, everyone gets along, and that's not interesting. We separate the types of conflict into two broad categories, external and internal conflict.

External conflict is a struggle between two opposing characters or forces. Internal conflict is a character with opposing desires. Both types are needed, and conflict must be visible and be able to be acted upon.

FAILURE

Though Bickham uses the term "disaster" in his structure theory, I prefer to use "Failure." Disaster suggests that the stakes are always super high, and they aren't always that high. Nor should they be.

Just like action, stakes rise and fall throughout a novel, and high stakes aren't necessarily better for a story. A small failure can sometimes be more useful to the story than a big one. Also, a failure can be a defeat, but it more often means that progress has been stopped, and the hero has to take a new course of action. The failure may be a verbal rebuke, a chance to steal a cheese sandwich, or an attempt to win the lottery. All failures lead to reactions.

SCENE STRUCTURE: PARTS OF ACTION & AFTERMATH—AFTERMATH

Newton's third law states that for every action, there is an equal and opposite reaction. If the scene Action is the action, then the Aftermath is the reaction. The parts of an Aftermath are **Reaction**, **Dilemma**, and **Decision**.

The easiest way to illustrate Aftermath is to describe step-by-step how it would happen in a scene. Let's say that the hero, Perkins, has a goal to pick daisies for his date (who is standing right next to him), but as soon as he reaches for the flowers, a bee lands on his hand. Perkins is allergic to bees. As in highly allergic, and the last time he was stung, he had to be rushed to the hospital. So he reacts by screaming, shaking his hand frantically, and wailing "Don't let them get me!" while sprinting to the nearest building for cover. Perkins has failed to pick the flowers.

DILEMMA

Once Perkins has reacted, he is faced with the chance to process what just happened, to plan a response, and to weigh the cost benefits of the response. This is not a slow sequence. If the hero is stung by the bee, the Aftermath will happen instantly as Perkins decides whether to seek medical or return to ask his date for help. If the bee doesn't sting him, then the Aftermath will be longer and more circumspect as the hero weighs the dilemma and its effect on him.

Should he return to his date and explain? Or should he disappear, too embarrassed by his freak-out? Really juicy dilemmas take a while to sort out. Ultimately, though, the hero does the cost-benefit mental analysis and proceeds to the decision.

DECISION

Having solved the dilemma, the hero decides on a new course of action, which will lead to the next scene. No matter how trivial it may seem, don't skip the decision! A character is created through their decisions. It is the moment where the character displays agency, and that agency leads to action. Action drives a story. If your beta reader, agent, or editor keep saying that your characters are too passive or that the plots are episodic, look closely at the decisions the characters are making. In passive novels, characters don't make decisions: Decisions are made for them. In active novels, characters make decisions and then act on them.

CHAPTERS VS. SCENES: WHY DOES IT MATTER?

The English word "chapter" comes via a circuitous route from the Latin word capitulum, which is the word that Romans used to head the sections of bound papyrus, which were separated as books (think the structure of the Bible, for example). A scroll of papyrus held 3000-5000 words, which is about the length of the chapters we read in novels today—even though books are not printed on scrolls made of swamp grass, and we are not bound by how many words we can squeeze onto a grass roll. It's a tradition that we seem to follow because maybe our attention spans are that long or we're just not creative enough to break them. Either way, we do seem to love our 35k chapters.

A few years ago, I was at a writers conference where the group was doing a revision exercise, and the person next to me turned to me and said, "What's the difference between a chapter and a scene?"

I replied, "Oh, that's easy, the difference between a chapter and a scene is...um..."

Intuitively, I knew the difference. I just couldn't articulate it. So I thought about it, read a bunch of books, and thought about it some more. This is what I came up with: scenes are decided by the story, and chapters are decided by the writer as a means of controlling the pace at which the reader reads the book. In other words, manipulation. I put the purposes of chapters for writers into three categories —reader pace, story pace, and reader engagement.

READER PACE: CONTROLLING THE SPEED OF READING

As I mentioned, the scene is for the story, and the chapter is for the reader. Why is the chapter for the reader? Because we want to control the reader's pace, how quickly or how slowly they move through our chapters. Writing so that the readers blow through all of the chapters is not necessarily a good thing. Even if you're writing a page-turner novel, sometimes you want to slow the pace down. Shorter chapters equal a faster reading pace. Longer chapters mean a slower reading pace. The reader gets a sense of moving through the book very quickly or very slowly. Sounds obvious, right? You may already be doing this on an intuitive level, so the next step is to be more intentional in your practice.

For task-oriented or easily distracted readers (and sometimes, for writers themselves), short chapters give a sense of accomplishment. For reluctant readers and those who struggle with fluency, short chapters keep them from getting bogged down. However, for methodical readers who like to immerse themselves in the reading, short chapters can be distracting and pull them out of the fictive dream. For readers who like to be immersed in the world, those quick chapters can be distracting. In this case, longer chapters might be preferable.

It's easy to see why knowing the audience is important for writers. Depending on the genre conventions, reader expectations vary greatly among readers. It makes it easier to get published if you follow those conventions, not to the letter but in general. It's good practice to always know the reader, and if you break a convention, make sure that you can do so with intention and a clear understanding of what you're trying to accomplish.

STORY PACE: BALANCING ACTION AND AFTERMATH

If you're using the Sticky Note process, you can clearly see the pace of a novel on the wall. Using the stickies, you can control pacing of the story by the way you proportion Action to Aftermath. If you see on the wall that a scene is heavy on events (Action) stickies and light on reflection (Aftermath) stickies, then you have made the story fast. Conversely, if the scene is light on action (scene) stickies and heavy on reflection (Aftermath) stickies, then the story pace is slower. Want to speed up a chapter? Take some of those reflection stickies down. Want to slow the pace? Add more reflection stickies. The more you add stickies to the wall, the slower the pace will be.

As you can tell from your wall, action/reflection effect has little to do with word count. The story in general won't slow down just because there are more words (as opposed to being wordy, which is different). Story events (Action) make the pace faster, even when the word count is high. Reflection (Aftermath) makes the pace slower, even when the word count is low.

By being intentional with the stickies, you can control the story pace of a scene by adjusting the balance of Action & Aftermath. Flexibility is important, though, so avoid taking a mechanical approach and don't try to shoehorn the novel into a prescribed pace.

Varying chapter lengths controls the rhythm of a story. All short chapters can feel choppy after a while. All long chapters can feel like a never-ending tome. If you want the story to move very quickly, shorten the chapters and format the paragraphs so that you use lots of white space. If you want the pace to move more slowly, create longer chapters and combine paragraphs to take out white space. Ink-dense paragraphs take longer to read.

We want the readers to feel like they're immersed in our world, and we want them to move at a certain pace for that to happen. Even if you're writing a page-turner, you don't want the same pace throughout the entire novel. Even if you're writing a literary novel, you want to give the reader a white space break once in a while. Most importantly, if you feel like the chapters are getting predictable and repetitive, change the pattern.

READER ENGAGEMENT: HOW TO REALLY HOOK READERS

We've all read a book that we just couldn't put down. There are many reasons a book can fit that description, but in general, it's because something kept readers turning the pages. We call this phenomenon reader engagement. Every writer wants to engage the reader. But how? One way to foster engagement is to structure chapters so that they hook the reader at the beginning and at the end. I call these ledes and kickers, which I've mentioned before. The purpose of ledes and kickers is to plant a question in the reader's mind, which compels them to seek an answer—and to keep reading.

SCENE STRUCTURE: LEDES AND KICKERS

As I mentioned earlier, the **lede** is the first sentence that shows the gist of the scene. It grounds the reader in the time and place of the scene, and if POV characters are switched at the chapter break, it tells us who has the POV. You can move the lede around, but unless the previous scene simply continues into this chapter, it helps to have it in the first or second paragraph. Ledes also steer the reader toward the new Scene Question.

Comparatively, a **kicker** comes at the end of a sentence and is often the last line. Although there are several types of kickers, the best known may be the cliffhanger. The term cliffhanger is considered to have gained fame when Thomas Hardy left one of his characters hanging from a cliff in the serial version of *A Pair of Blue Eyes.* Hardy kept his readers in suspense until the next serial segment was published, probably to generate more sales. Many other authors of classic and contemporary novels have used the cliffhanger.

No surprise there: Cliffhangers are very effective. However, if you use too many of them, they lose their effect. After a couple of kickers that imperil a character, the reader will recognize the gimmick and stop caring. Like paragraph length and the use of white space, it's best to mix things up when it comes to kickers.

Remember Moose from earlier in this book, the pound rescue dog with gorgeous fur and jacked-up teeth? We're going to do a series of kickers starring Moose to show there are many other types of kickers that you can use, including the following:

- End with a cliffhanger: by now, you know exactly what a cliffhanger is: *Moose saw the child disappear as he ran toward the edge of the cliff, and without a second of hesitation, he leapt...*
- Let a character ask a question: A question begs an answer. Denying that answer is an effective way to cause the reader to keep reading: *Moose had wandered for six weeks through the Rocky Mountains, following some primal instinct that led him. Was this the way home? Would he ever find it?*
- Push a stranger in the story: Everyone is familiar with stranger danger. Adding a stranger to a scene adds danger, along with a dose of the unknown. *Moose had spent the first weeks of his life in the shelter. One by one, he had seen his brothers and sisters adopted until he was the last of the litter. With his jacked-up teeth and funky hips, he was always passed by, invisible. Then one morning, the door opened, and a new girl walked in. She was short and blonde*

and smiled so big when she looked into his cage, it felt like she saw him.

- Correlate an object. Give special qualities to an object in the story, such as a diamond ring, a locket, or a baseball glove. Later on, endow that object with memories, emotions, and a past. This is often called an objective correlative, which is a group of things that come to define the emotions of a character. T.S Eliot defined it in this way: 'The only way of expressing emotion in the form of art is by finding an 'objective correlative;' in other words, a set of objects, a situation, a chain of events which shall be the formula of that 'particular' emotion; such that when the external facts, which must terminate in sensory experience, are given, the emotion is immediately evoked." That's a long way of saying an object that is correlated to a character's emotional state. *The girl held a blue shiny thing, shaped like a bone. She clipped it to Moose's collar and said, "Now everyone will know your name is Moose, and if you ever get lost, they will know just how to reach me."*

- Drop a clue. So if you're doing a mystery and you've suddenly revealed a clue, the reader wants to know how it fits into the puzzle. *A rustling noise woke Moose, but before he could focus in the dark, he felt a sharp stab in his flank. Then something heavy fell over his head, and he felt his collar unclip. He was lifted by strong hands and dropped onto something hard and metal. Car doors slammed, and he heard an engine start. He shook his head, feeling groggy, and there was no sound, no clink of the blue-boned tag.*

- Plant a red herring: This works for more than just mystery novels. It's like anything else: You don't know something. But you have a piece of information, and you turn the page to find out what the mystery is. *Moose took a deep sniff and caught a familiar scent. It was sharp and burned his nose, but he had smelled it somewhere close to home, on someone, but his head was fuzzy, and he couldn't quite remember who.*

- Reveal a secret: A character has been hiding something from another character or the reader. Share the secret and see what happens. *The plump cat stared hard at Moose, then as if he had passed some test, rolled over, revealing a shiny blue thing under its belly. The girl's metal bone!*

- Create an epiphany: Ever seen that old commercial when an actor would smack themselves and say, "I could've had a V8?" I don't know why anyone would want a V8, but that sudden realization is an example of an epiphany. *Moose woke up in a crate. Not his crate, but a metal one with thick bars. When he looked outside, he expected to see the flat Kansas cornfields stretching out for miles, but instead, he saw high mountains blocking out the sky. That's when the thought struck him—my girl is gone.*

- Break the scene in media res. If I have a scene that's going on too long, I may just insert a chapter break in the middle of it. It's a really annoying technique to use, but it's often effective because the reader's like, what just happened? *When the hands reached down to unlock the crate, Moose kept his eyes closed. He waited until the door swung free and the hands reached for his throat, then his eyes popped open. And so did his jaws.*

- Come out of left field. Something happens for no reason whatsoever. Weird? Yes. Effective? Absolutely. *Moose heard the growl and froze at the edge of the road. He looked up, barely able to lift his head, and saw the coyote, hackles raised, jaws open, pacing sideways, sizing him up. Another growl so loud it was almost deafening, then the coyote leapt— straight into the side of a big metal thing (to us humans, a truck).*

- Set a goal: Goals are good because every character can pursue a goal, even canines. *Moose stood on the edge of the canyon. The sun was an orange ball, going down behind the mountains. He was exhausted and hungry and wanted nothing more than to lie down. He started to do it, to spend the night here in the sinking sun...Sun! That was it. All he had to do was walk toward the orange light, and it would show him the way.*

ACTIVITIES
DIGGING DEEPER

It took writing six novels to wrap my brain around scene structure. Maybe it's because the terms befuddled me. Maybe it's because I confused scenes with chapters. Or maybe it's because I'm just not very good with theory. I like to know how a thing is made.

Many writers have attempted to explicate scene structure. Most of their explanations didn't resonate with me. In *The Art of Fiction*, John Gardner wrote that a scene is "an unbroken flow of action without a lapse of time or leap from one setting to another." Great definition but not one that helped me build a scene. It all clicked when I realized that scenes are interconnected.

- Scenes don't exist by and of themselves. The structure of a scene is partially created by the ending of the scene before.
- Some strands run throughout an entire novel. Those strands are picked up by a new scene, woven in, and left for the scene that follows.
- Once I understood the connectedness of scenes, the minutiae of structure became easier to see. When I sticky

note scenes now, I understand the multiple jobs they
have to do to move the story forward.

- That's what writing scenes is about—breaking things
  into parts and then putting them back together to form a
  cohesive whole.
- Somewhere in the middle of that mechanical process,
  there is artistry. It's hard to define and impossible to
  pinpoint, but don't let the machine keep you from seeing
  the ghost inside.

EXERCISE 1

Let's apply this exercise to your current work in progress. Open your
favorite novel to the first page of a random chapter. Without looking
back to the previous page, write a kicker that would have made you
want to read the current scene. Then, without looking at the end of
the chapter, write the kicker that ends the scene. Compare what
you've written to what the author wrote. Which is better?

EXERCISE 2

Stakes are what a character has to lose or gain in a scene. Building
stakes is a hurdle for many writers. Luckily, the Sticky Note Plot
method makes it easier to see the stakes in action. As I mentioned
earlier, brainstorming on your sticky wall is a great way to generate a
list of stakes. Try this: Open your work in progress to a random chapter. Find the things that are at stake for the POV character. Make a
stack of stickies of the things you found. On the sticky note, cross out
each word on the list and replace it with an elevated stake. If the
character stands to gain money, triple the amount. If they are about
to lose a promotion, make it their job. Can you elevate every stake in
the scene? What effect does it have on conflict, tension, and character's desire line? When you're done, put the stickies on the wall.

STICKY NOTE CHECKLIST: SCENE STRUCTURE

- Most scenes are made of three components: Exposition, Precursors, and Action & Aftermath.
- Action & Aftermath are a coupled sequence used to advance the action of a story.
- Exposition is the connective tissue that provides context and meaning to the action and reactions of Action & Aftermath.
- If you get confused by the term Action & Aftermath, think of the concept as "action & reaction" or "cause & effect." Remember Newton's Third Law.
- Scenes are building blocks of a story.
- Chapters are formatted to control the reader's access to the story.
- Action & Aftermath can happen at a macro level in a scene. It can also happen at the micro level in a paragraph, sentence, or even in dialogue.
- Kickers may seem like a gimmick to get the reader to turn the page, but they are vital for setting up the next scene and keeping your reader engaged.

CHAPTER 9
SCENE STRUCTURE REVISION

OUR NEXT ROUND OF REVISION DOESN'T use your manuscript itself. It doesn't use that many stickies either. What? I know, right? But we will return to plastering the wall with stickies later on. For this next round, we are not going to go in and begin editing lines. There will be no line notes. There will be no copy editing. There will be no shifting of scenes from one place to the next. There will be no additions of witty dialogue, insightful interior monologue, none of that. We're only going to use your manuscript as a reference.

Much of the information that you read in this chapter will be a repeat of information presented earlier in the book. That is intentional. In the previous chapter, I explained and defined the vocabulary that we're going to be using in this section chapter. Now, we're going to put theory into practice.

As you do the exercises below, the same info is available to you, with even more explication, so that you have a firm idea of what to write down. Revising a novel is a complex undertaking, and it sometimes takes multiple explanations of concepts before they sink in, especially concepts that have to do with revision.

THE SPREADSHEET OF DOOM: SOME CALL IT MAGIC

At this point, we're going to open something that I affectionately call the Spreadsheet of Doom (SSOD), which is my scene structure sheet. It is the primary tool I use to do an intense, laborious, but necessary entire novel revision pass. Using the spreadsheet will likely be an unpleasant process. It may frustrate you and challenge you. To me, it's a form of torture, which is why I call it the Spreadsheet of Doom. Of course, you can write an entire novel without ever using this spreadsheet or taking these steps. But in the long run, life will be easier—and the revision process will be more thorough—if you do. Even if you hate it as much as I do!

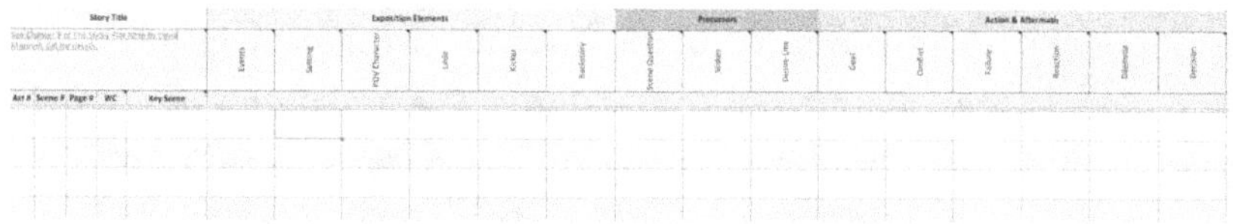

THE SPREADSHEET OF DOOM

The Spreadsheet of Doom began as a simple spreadsheet that helped me track what happens in each scene. While Word and Scrivener are excellent tools for writing the entire novel in one document, it is difficult to track the essential elements of each scene just by looking at those scenes on paper or the computer screen. And frankly, when you're getting granular, the Sticky Note Wall becomes too cluttered.

You can download a FREE copy of the SSOD by signing up for the Sticky Note Plotletter at stickynoteplot.com

So I developed a spreadsheet to keep track of action, setting, ledes, which POV character was featured in the scene and a few other elements. Over time, the spreadsheet expanded until it became something of a behemoth that allowed me to track almost every element in the story. Filling it out can be one of the most rewarding exercises I do. The difficulty is it takes time to do it. Lots of time.

The advantage of using the SSOD is it forces us to recognize the missing elements in the novel and it gives you a chance to put them in. What if, right now, let's say you have a work in progress with roughly 80 to 90 scenes, and you're feeling pretty good about those scenes as is. I would guess that 30 percent of those scenes don't need to be in the novel. They don't have characters that make decisions. There's no scene question and answer. The stakes are very low. The action doesn't drive the story forward or the exposition doesn't add anything that the reader needs to know to understand the story. If you were to remove such a scene completely from the novel, the novel would still stand.

So you may have written three thousand words when the reader only needs three hundred of those words. We are often told in revision to find the scenes that are weak, but we're seldom told what makes a scene weak. Filling out the SSOD will make those weaknesses obvious to you. It will also show you the scenes that are strong, not just in the action but in the elements that the scene needs in order to make the story successful.

Ready to start?

Let's begin with a story title.

SPREADSHEET CATEGORIES

We start the SSOD by creating a title for your novel. Titles are important in the early drafts because they help us define the story in our minds. Be aware that the title may change. It is not uncommon for the publisher to change the title when they buy a book because they see it as a different product than the author may. When I was working on *Soul Enchilada*, I had a completely different working title. I sold the novel under a second title. Then we changed it to a third title to make the book more marketable. That working title was very important for me because it was funny. It had many dark elements that could have gone badly, and I needed to remember that *Soul Enchilada* was meant to be a fun book.

The same is true of my second published novel *Black Hole Sun*. That was not the first title. *Mars Stinks* was the working title, and that's the opening line of the book. I never intended the title to be *Mars Stinks*. It was a placeholder until something better came along. Something better came from an unexpected source, the video game *Rock Band*. My family loved playing *Rock Band*, and one of the songs that we played a ton was Soundgarden's "Black Hole Sun." I loved the trippy deep feeling of the arrangement, the way it made me feel like the walls were closing in. That sonic claustrophobia captured the essence of my novel's setting, so I made the switch. I thought it was a really cool title too. Luckily, my editor agreed.

Having said all of that, what a publisher might do doesn't matter at this point. Just write in a working title for the book. We have to start somewhere. Once you have the working title, type it into the SSOD and write it on a sticky note. Put the note on the wall so that you can always see it.

STORY: LOGLINES, ACT, SCENE #, PAGE#, WORD COUNT, AND SCENE TYPE

Under the story title is a space for a logline. A logline is the Hollywood phrase for a short description of a movie, which allows someone to quickly understand the gist of the story. The logline doesn't list every element of the story, but it acts as a preview, making you want to experience that movie.

A logline for a novel has the same kind of information, and it has the same goal— to make you buy the book. You will find loglines in publications that list new sales of novels. If you write a good logline, publishers will sometimes use the logline in editorial meetings, sales meetings, and promotional materials. A great logline will make selling the book much easier for you, for your agent, for your editor, and ultimately even for the bookseller,

But right now, we don't care about the commercial aspects of longlining. We care about finishing the novel so that we can sell it, and that's when a logline becomes a crucial element of revision. An excellent logline contains the key story elements of a novel—premise, hero, dilemma, stakes, villain, and story goals. It summarizes in a nutshell the core of the story, and before you begin revising the story, you have to know what it's truly about.

HOW TO WRITE A LOGLINE FOR YOUR NOVEL AND PUT IT ON STICKY NOTE

As I said, a logline (or log line) is a one-to-three-sentence descriptor of a story. It gets its name, I have heard, from a time when someone had to log each storyline, and they wanted to write as little as possible. Or maybe studio heads wanted to read as little as possible. No matter how they started, loglines are an ingrained part of the movie industry and now, the publishing world, as well.

Loglines are very useful to you, the author. They allow you to answer the question "So what's your book about?" with a succinct phrase, rather than beginning with "Well, see there's this guy...."

A second good use for the logline is the pitch, which is the pitch you would make to an editor on, say, an elevator. You've only got seconds to spit out the premise of your novel, and it has to be convincing. This handy, dandy quick summary of the story is very useful in persuading agents, editors, and even the dentist that you've hit on a "wow" premise that simply must be written.

The third use—the one that matters most for the SSOD—is for you. A novel is a big thing. It's difficult to hold the whole story in your mind, especially when you've finished a first draft and are still giddy from the flow of creative juices. Writing a logline helps you define—for yourself—the essential elements of the plot. It will also let you know immediately what major components of the plot are missing. This prevents episodic plots that are a string of (interesting and exciting) events that lack a complete story spine.

Here's a template for a logline:

Given situation A, then Our Hero does action B despite complication C while antagonist D tries to stop Our Hero by doing E before F can happen.

This is a simple template, not an ironclad rule (as you'll notice below, my loglines don't match this exactly). The template is broken into six components. Each represents a specific part of the story.

A: *Given situation A*...This is the state of things as the novel begins, or it may be an action that occurs at the very beginning of the story to incite the action. Think of it as a boulder poised on the edge of a cliff, needing just a little nudge to set it rolling.

B: *Then Our Hero does action*...The boulder is about to roll or is rolling already, and it's Our Hero's job to stop it. Or divert it. Or pick it up and fling it like a marble across the Mojave Desert. It doesn't matter what Our Hero does, just as long as they act.

1. *Despite complication C*...Plot is complication. Character development is conflict. The two should go hand in hand to prevent Our Hero from acting. It can be a physical incapacity. Or a geographical space. Or a personal relationship. Just as long as it slows Our Hero down and makes it that much more difficult to stop that rolling boulder.

2. *While antagonist D tries to stop Our Hero*...Make life easy and include a villain in the story. It's much easier to ensure complication and conflict if there is another character working in direct opposition to Our Hero. Don't want a villain or can't think of one? Circumstances, time, distance, society, and geography can be strong enough forces to stop Our Hero, although it's more difficult to pull off.

3. *By doing E...*Our Hero has been acting to stop that boulder. Our Villain is also acting to stop Our Hero, and it looks like the villain will succeed. So long, boulder.

4. *Before F can happen...*In this case, F would be the dire circumstances that face Our Hero and others if Our Hero fails. The chance of failure must be real, and almost certain, for the story to have drama.

Here are some examples of novels I've written. These are real loglines I wrote to convince a publisher to buy the book. Some of the loglines are better than others.

- For *Soul Enchilada*: It's 'Faust Meets Men in Black' in this YA paranormal about a teen girl who must risk her soul to keep Lucifer from repossessing her most treasured possession, the 1958 Cadillac Biarritz she inherited from her dearly departed grandfather.
- For *Black Hole Sun*: On a terraformed Mars, where teenaged soldiers sell their services to the highest bidder, sixteen-year-old Durango and his crew must fight a band of marauding cannibals to protect a destitute mining outpost—and the dark secret they keep.

Now it's your turn. Use the template to create your own logline but remember to play with it so that the line is something you can memorize and feel comfortable saying to another person. Even on an elevator. With a boulder rolling toward you.

Got it? Now, write your logline on a sticky note and plop it on the Wall above your other stickies. Write the logline on a second sticky and put it on your computer screen. Keep it there for the entire process of writing the novel. If you lose your way or get caught in the weeds, you can look at the sticky and be reminded of the essence of the story. It helps you find your way back.

Under logline on the SSOD, you'll find columns for act number, scene number, and page number, word count, and Key Scene. The act number will be Act 1, Act 2A, the Turn, Act 2B, or Act 3. The scene number is the sequential number of scenes, so you will enter Scene 1, Scene 2, etc. Notice that there are no chapter numbers. That's because, I believe, chapters are artificial segmentations that have nothing to do with the writing process. Page number is obvious. We include the number of pages to show when the scene begins and when it ends. By putting the word count for each scene, you'll be able to see how long the scenes are at a glance.

If you have not already, write every scene question and every scene goal and put them on the wall. Ignore the clutter for now.

Once you finish the SSOD, you can even use the graphing feature to chart the length of all the scenes. Note that at this point, there's no place to keep a running total for the whole novel word count. During revision, I'm not concerned with the overall length of the novel. If it's too long at the end of SSOD revision, I can cut pages. Cutting pages is easier than creating new ones.

Finally, there's a column for the Key Scenes. I type a description of every Key Scene into the spreadsheet. If a scene is one of the Key Scenes, type in the kind of Key Scene. If it's not a Key Scene, type in an uppercase R for regular. There are two types of scenes, regular scenes and Key Scenes. Regular scenes are necessary to building a story, but they can be removed without affecting the overall structure. If you pull that scene out, it doesn't yank out a tent pole the story needs. Key scenes are crucial to the overall structure of the story, so those Key Scenes have to be in there. Do not cut them without replacing them.

ELEMENTS: ACTION, SETTING, POV, CHARACTER, LEDE, KICKER, AND BACKSTORY

Whew! So much typing! Remember, our goal is to fill in every, single box in the SSOD. Now, we move on to the second segment on the SSOD, the **exposition elements**. These are the mechanics of the scene, the combination of elements that the reader can see on the page. It is the apparatus for the physical structure of the scene. Like key scenes, these elements are necessary.

EVENTS

The first **element** is the **events** of the scene. We write down the events for a couple of reasons. One reason is to remind us of what's happening when we review the SSOD. What did the protagonists do in this scene? What was the action of the plot? How did the hero move forward? Type a one-sentence summary of the action into the spreadsheet.

The other reason is to make sure that characters do something in every scene. If there's a scene with a very long **aftermath**—where the character is primarily internal and processing information, they should be doing something, even if it's just making a cup of coffee and sitting down to read the newspaper. If there's a scene with the character in their head the entire time, it's not really a scene. It's just a vignette of interior monologue.

SETTING

Scenes may have multiple **settings**. Characters can move around, both in space and time. Just because you changed the setting, it doesn't mean that you changed the scene. Try to establish the scene in the first or second paragraph of a new scene using a lede because in addition to having a scene question for the hero, a scene has to ground the reader in time and place.

Every story has a world, and the author has to build the world for the reader. It doesn't matter if the setting is contemporary, historical, fantasy, or futuristic, the world has to be built. The most direct way to do that is through exposition, but no one wants to churn through huge chunks of exposition, so we have to slide the exposition in slyly, almost so that the reader doesn't notice it. One way to accomplish this is to have characters moved physically through the setting and adding small, telling details that flesh out the setting. Hemingway was a master at this. He wrote contemporary literary fiction, but his techniques can teach us, no matter what genre we write. Don't stop the action for an info dump or description. Keep the action moving. The easiest way to do that is to have the character move or interact with a setting.

Once you've established the scene, you can use shorthand to cue the reader in that you're in the same places you've been before. It's important to do this at the beginning of the scene so that the reader knows where they are. It seems like a small thing to us as novelists, but by reminding the character of time in place, we ground them very quickly and it allows us to move on with the story. We don't confuse the reader with questions that they should have answers to. The last thing we want to do is make our reader feel as if they are in a time warp or floating in space.

A note about setting (and an explanation of why I'm making a big deal of it right now): As I mentioned earlier, many beginning authors try to remove setting from a story, thinking that giving a sparse setting or no setting at all means that the story can place it take place anywhere.

No.

A story that takes place anywhere takes place nowhere, and you probably get a negative reaction from the reader. They won't feel as if the time and place in your novel are universal. They will probably feel as if they're floating in the ether, unattached to any place or time. So choose the setting wisely. Try to make it an important component of the novel. Have the characters interact with it and make it part of the story itself. The more you ground the reader in a place, the more you can use a sense of place to enhance the psychological and emotional aspects of the story. As long as the themes are universal, the reader will feel as if the story is universal. So...don't skip the setting column! Write a shorthand description of the setting for each scene. Got multiple scenes in the same setting? Cut and paste the description to save time.

POINT OF VIEW CHARACTER

The next column is **point of view character**. It's important to keep track of the POV character. If you're writing a straightforward novel in only one POV and in the same verb tense throughout, then this is a column that's easily filled out. Just bulk-fill it with the hero's name. However, if the novel is told using multiple viewpoints, including an omniscient POV, you have to track which character is delivering the narrative. You can also track switches of point of view during a scene.

LEDE

The next column is the **lede**. I cut and paste the entire lede into this column. The lede is the sentence that delivers the gist of a scene. It is often one of the first sentences of the scene, though the lede can also be a "delayed lede," which comes later in the scene in the form of a more interesting hook.

When we authors begin a new chapter or scene, our first instinct may be to simply continue the action from the previous chapter, as if the chapter break or scene break did not matter. There is nothing wrong with this instinct, and it is possible to write an effective novel using this kind of sequential structure all the way through. Sometimes, though, it makes it easier for us and the reader if we move out of chronological sequence.

In his craft book, *Writing the Novel from Plot to Print*, Lawrence Block calls this strategy **First Things Second**. He tells the story of an editor who after reading one of his early manuscripts told him to switch his first and second chapters. The first chapter was full of exposition of world-building, explaining the character's background information. The second chapter was about a murder, and the hero then set out to solve the mystery. Following his editor's advice, Block swapped the second chapter for the first, thus beginning the novel with the hook (the murder). The chapter that had been Chapter One became Chapter Two, and it answered all of the questions that were blooming in the reader's mind as they read the first chapter.

We can do the same thing with a scene. Is the new scene's lede a big paragraph of exposition, followed by a paragraph full of juicy bits of action? Swap the paragraphs. Start with the action, then follow with the lede. If you're concerned that the scene opening isn't strong enough, consider using a First Things Second lede to set the hook.

KICKER

The next column is **kicker**. As you know, a kicker is the last line of a scene that figuratively kicks the reader into the next scene. Tracking the kickers reminds you to:

1. Have one
2. Vary the type of kickers used.

I cut and paste the entire kicker into this column. Some users of the SSOD record the type of kicker in this column, as well as the kicker itself.

BACKSTORY

Like medicine, **backstory** is best when delivered in the smallest dose possible, as close to when the reader needs it. It would be the fictive equivalent to the Just-in-Time (JIT) inventory model, which was invented by Toyota. The car company only orders goods right before they are needed. No inventory is left waiting around to be used. Now think about a just-in-time inventory model in terms of how to deliver the information the reader needs: we only give to them right before they need it, not several chapters previously.

If backstory is written in the form of a flashback, it works better if the exposition is triggered by a memory or physical action or endowed object in the story. This is a good place to create objective correlatives (also known as objects endowed with emotions) that have psychological meaning and connect parts of the story. Backstory gets a bad name, and frankly, it deserves it.

Many writers frontload the beginning of a novel, especially the first scene, giving information that the reader does not need at that moment. It's the fallacy that the reader needs to know as much about the characters as they do. Save that information until it's needed. Parcel it out over the course of the story. Think of backstory like salt: A little is terrific and enhances the flavor of the story. Too much is overwhelming and destroys the enjoyment. So unless the reader needs the backstory immediately, save it for later or my preference, cut it out all. Unless the backstory has a specific reason to be in a scene, leave it out.

If it needs to be in the scene, type it into the cell but don't go it great detail. Save that for the manuscript.

PRECURSORS: SCENE Q & A, STAKES, AND DESIRE LINES

The next section of scene structure elements are **precursors**. Precursors are scene elements that aren't visible in the writing on the paper and were set in place by previous scenes. They are agitations that form a chain reaction in the story. Most of the time, pre-cursors exist between the lines unless the hero explicitly states a scene question or scene goal—which is sometimes the case.

Unlike other elements, you may not be able to put a finger on precursors, but they are necessary. The most important precursor is the scene question and its accompanying scene answer. These two are essential non-negotiable elements in every scene. You really, really need a scene question, often referred to in craft books as a dramatic question. Without a scene question, there's no reason for the scene to exist in the story. There are several possible answers to a scene question. Yes, no, yes but, yes and, no and, no but, and no plus.

Remember, if the answer to the scene question is just plain "yes," it's time to change the scene question. In any novel, there is one central story question, and it is asked early on, before the end of the first couple of chapters. It is usually something like, what is wrong in the world and how is the hero going to fix it? The central story question is not the only question. Smaller questions lead up to it and are generated by it.

At the scene level, there are also dramatic questions. It is the scene question the reader has in mind when they begin the chapter. The purpose of the scene is to attempt to answer that question. Scene questions can be as simple as, "Will Kasha finish her homework?" Or as complicated as, "Will they kiss?" Or as deadly as, "Will the time bomb in the bus explode?" No matter how high-stakes the question is, the events of the scene are about the characters acting to answer the question.

STAKES

The next precursor is **stakes**. Previously, I asked you to brainstorm many possible stakes. Now it's time to choose the best ones. Type them into the spreadsheet. Now ask yourself again, what is at stake in the scene? As you know, stakes can be both internal and external. External site stakes are often what's at stake for the characters' physical being, while internal stakes are often what's at stake for the character's emotions. What kind of stakes are in this specific scene?

DESIRE LINE

Every hero has a **desire line**. It unites the story. It is the equivalent of the plot line for the story. It weaves its way through every scene, changing based on the events of each scene. What does the character yearn to have? What are they willing to give up to get it? How does the desire line change as the story progresses? How does the character transform throughout each scene, throughout the story? How does the desire line unite the character's goals, actions, and stakes? These questions are vital for clarifying the desire line, but then answers can be nebulous or convoluted. Since you can't type a nebulous, convoluted answer in a tiny spreadsheet cell, it's important to be able to articulate a character's desire line as clearly as you can articulate a logline.

ACTION & AFTERMATH: GOAL, CONFLICT, FAILURE, REACTION, DILEMMA, AND DECISION

We move on to the last segment on the SSOD, the **action & aftermath**. When you fill out this section, some of the information will probably overlap with info you put under the precursors and elements. Earlier, we talked about the theory of action & aftermath. Now we're going to apply the concepts of action & aftermath to your novel using the SSOD.

GOAL

A main character's **scene goal** is specific and obvious to the reader. It is connected to the **Scene Q&A**. The character goal leads to the answer to the scene question. The scene question and scene goal are often the exact same thing. However, there are some scenes where the scene question is not answered by the POV character's goal. I make the distinction like this: the scene question is what the reader wants to know. The scene goal is what the character wants to accomplish. Write every scene goal on a sticky and put it on your wall.

CONFLICT

External conflict is a struggle between two opposing characters or forces. **Internal conflict** is a character with opposing desires. Both are needed. External conflict must be visible and must be able to be acted upon. Conflict is very important to a whole novel, especially at the beginning, because it sets up a **scene question** that must be answered. But conflict is just as important to each scene. In some ways, it's like having micro conflict and macro conflict. Note: as you read about the different forms of conflict, think about how you would write that conflict on

a sticky. If you can't think of any conflicts in the scene, this is a good place to use stickies to brainstorm ideas.

Macro-conflicts are conflicts that arise throughout the novel and are solved by the big events of the story. Micro-conflicts are small conflicts that begin in a scene and are often resolved during the scene.

Micro-conflicts can be simple things—a character who wants a piece of pie and the other character who has already called dibs on it. Or a character who needs to go to the bathroom but is being prevented from it. A character who wants to say one thing, but they are squelched by the other characters and their running conversations. In a scene, look for the micro-conflicts that will just make things a little bit harder for the characters. Conflict happens in the moment when another character is pushing against the hero, or when the hero is pushing against another character. The main conflict for the hero comes from the antagonistic force that we call the villain. Don't think that conflict is only between the hero and the antagonist. At any point in the story, it can arise from multiple places.

The hero may interact with mentor characters who have the same goal and support them in their goal. Think of Obi-Wan Kenobi, who pushes Luke Skywalker to accept his fate. The hero character may have a love interest that's a source of conflict. The hero may have a sidekick who is a source of conflict. The hero may have people in their life who are encouraging them to behave a certain way. That's a source of conflict, too.

Internal conflict is when the character is at war with themselves. They want two different things, usually things that they cannot have at the same time. Sometimes, this is a moral conflict, but internal conflict can be a small scale as well: *I want a donut.* You can't have a donut. *I want a donut.* You can't have a donut. You said you're going to stop eating donuts. *I'm going to eat a donut.* No, you're not.

That's interior internal conflict. Now that's a very simplified example, and you can find other, better ones. When you do, type them into the spreadsheet. Put them on the wall.

FAILURE

Failure is all about the stakes in the scene and the character's inability to overcome those stakes. Stakes don't have to keep climbing throughout a novel. There are certain genres like thrillers where the stakes get higher and higher as the novel progresses, or they start out high and they continue to be high. In most fiction, stakes rise and fall.

There are also small stakes at play in each scene. A small setback in a chapter can be more useful to a story than a big one. That's why failure is important—because we need to see how a character responds after failing. How do they deal with the consequences? Do they curl up in a fetal ball and ask for a nice safe cage? Or do they double down on their resolve and vow to keep striving? Type the action of their failure into the spreadsheet.

REACTION

Now we're into the **aftermath** part of the scene. If the scene is the action, the aftermath is the reaction. After the hero fails, they react to the failure. If they get kicked in the face, their head jerks back, his lips get busted, and they fall down. All of that is reaction, but the hero doesn't have to get kicked in order to react. Failures lead to reactions.

DILEMMA

Once the hero has reacted, they are faced with a **dilemma**. They have the chance to review the scene events, to plan a response, and to weigh the benefits of a response. The Aftermath will happen very quickly as the hero decides whether to give in or attack other times. Ultimately, the hero does their mental analysis and proceeds. The hero decides on a new course of action which will lead to the next scene.

DECISION

This new course of action is a **decision**. That decision is absolutely necessary. That's because the character has to show agency. Agency means that the character owns their decisions. They have the power to make them, and they have the capacity to act upon them. If the character never makes a decision, they are being pulled through the story, rather than pushing their way through it. If you are someone who is told that they write passive characters, that your stories are episodic in nature, or that they're too quiet, take a look at the decisions the characters are making. Active characters make goals, and they act on those goals. Passive characters wait and wonder. They wish, they hope, but they don't do. This means that they depend upon the other characters in the novel to pull them through their own story.

We want to read about heroes. We want to hear about people who overcome the obstacles that we face and cannot overcome. We want someone larger than life, even if it's only a little bit larger than life. We want a hero who can say the things that we can't say and do the things that we dare not do. The point in the story when that hero is made is right here at the end of the Aftermath where they decide to act. Make sure every one of the scenes has an Aftermath and that every one of those Aftermaths ends with a decision to move forward.

Hey! You've finished the first row of the SSOD, and you have all the necessary info about Scene One. Now go on to Scene Two. Then Three. Keep going until you fill out a row for every scene. If you don't know a scene question, goal, etc. you can skip it for now. Eventually, though, you have to find out what you don't know.

THE DOUGHNUT HOLE

Now we are finished with the SSOD, and for this round, we're done putting new stickies on the wall. You've filled out most spreadsheet cells for most scenes. But you're exhausted, and your brain wants a rest. We will give it one. The left side, anyway. We're going to use the right side for this next step.

It's time to step back and look at both the SSOD and the Sticky Note Wall in a meta-visual way. We want to pull back so that we can't read the individual spreadsheet cells or sticky notes. Shrink the spreadsheet on your computer screen so that you can see the whole thing. Step away from the Sticky Note Wall so that you see only the pattern of the stickies.

See that? Right in the middle of the SSOD and the Sticky Note Wall, there is a hole. I call it the Doughnut Hole. The hole is formed by all the things you don't know about the story. Usually, you can fill out the row completely for the scenes in Act 1. You can do the same for Act 3. Then uh-oh, the closer you get to the Turn, the less you seem to know about the scene. There's a big blank space in the middle of the SSOD and in the Sticky Note Wall.

To quote Douglas Adams, don't panic. Just fill in the missing spaces.

Nope, I'm not kidding or being sarcastic. The Turn is an essential part of the plot and the character arc. You have to know it before you can go on. So take as long as you need to complete the Spreadsheet.

Use stickies to brainstorm ideas. Retrace the character's arc. Find some backstory that increases the dramatic tension of the blank scenes. The ideas will come. Give it time. And when you filled in cells, when you've turned the Doughnut Hole into a jelly-filled doughnut full of sweet goodness, you're ready for the next step.

LETTING THE JELLY DOUGHNUT MARINADE

Okay, so the idea of a doughnut floating in a marinade is not the most appetizing in the world, but that's still what has to happen. Not that you're finished with SSOD, it's time to set the whole novel aside. If you're sighing with relief, thumbs up. You deserve a rest after all the hard work you've done. If you're about to lose your mind over the idea of pausing while you're on a hot streak, keep reading so that I can convince you.

Here's the good news: you're almost done with the Spreadsheet of Doom and with this round of sticky notes. You can throw the stickies away again—except for the logline on your computer. Keep that one.

The next step is to open your draft document to Scene One. Compare the information written in the SSOD to the manuscript. Look for each story element in the scene. If it is present in the scene, mark the SSOD in some way so that the element is present. You can change the color of the cell or just put a note next to the info. Your choice. If the element is not present, write it into the scene. Don't just make a note of it. Write it into the action of the scene. Keep doing that, scene by scene, until you have completed the steps for every scene. This may take a while. Keep at it. It will benefit you so much later. Let's fast-forward ahead to the point where you've finished putting the SSOD elements into each and every scene. You're maybe exhausted and a little burned out. Hang on. There's a time to rest coming soon.

Here's the next and final step of the SSOD revision: Print out the SSOD. Print out the manuscript. Take them both and put them away.

It's the old idea of "out of sight, out of mind." The manuscript will be out of sight. The story, though, is alive in your head. It's growing and changing, making connections, and pulling up backstory that you would never have in your conscious mind.

Megan Whalen Turner calls this process "putting it under the bed," although she literally puts it under her bed. I don't think you have to go that far, but I do think it's a good idea to set novels aside once the first draft is finished so that your subconscious can work on them for you while you set to work on the next thing—y'know the shiny, new story idea that was tempting you while you were working on the novel. In the meantime, keep a stack of stickies around. If inspiration strikes, write it down. Collect all of these ideas until we're ready to build our final Sticky Note Wall.

ACTIVITIES
DIGGING DEEPER

The SSOD can be overwhelming. While it contains all of the important information about every scene in your working draft, the purpose of what you're doing may not be clear. The purpose of the SSOD is to double-check that every scene has what it needs to work.

However, writing the information in the SSOD or putting it on the Sticky Note Wall doesn't insert that information in the novel. You will do that in the next round of revision. In the meantime, we can focus on the element that we started the SSOD with, the logline. Since the logline serves so many purposes, it's not a bad idea to practice making them.

EXERCISE 1

Write a logline for your current work in progress. The draft doesn't need to be completed to write a good logline. What does the logline tell you about your plot?

EXERCISE 2

Write a logline for an idea for a novel that's been percolating for a while. Or even three half-baked ideas you've been wondering about whether it's worth working on or not. It's not necessary to have a draft or even a Sticky Note Plot Wall done. A premise is enough. If you can write a logline that makes someone go *wow*, then it has enough juice to turn into a novel.

STICKY NOTE CHECKLIST: SCENE STRUCTURE REVISION

- The Spreadsheet of Doom is my primary tool for an entire novel revision.
- Using the spreadsheet will likely be an unpleasant process. It may frustrate you and challenge you.
- Loglines allow an author to answer the question, "so what's your book about?" succinctly.
- Loglines create handy, dandy quick elevator pitch for agents, editors, and even the dentist.
- Loglines define the essential elements of the plot and let you know if major components of the plot are missing.
- Precursors are in place before a scene begins.
- Expect a Doughnut Hole even after finishing the Spreadsheet of Doom. The spreadsheet is meant to show you everything that's missing from the manuscript. Keep combining and revising scenes until the hole is filled.

PART 4

SPIT & POLISH

CHAPTER 10
CHARACTERS, DIALOGUE, AND STYLE

HEY, REMEMBER THAT MANUSCRIPT MARINATING under the bed? It's time to take it out and not read it. Well, you're going to read it, but not in the same way you'd read a completed novel written by someone else. This time, you're going to make a polishing pass for character and only character, focusing on character arcs.

It's also time to build our final Sticky Note Wall. As you read, write the usual things on the stickies—action, conflict, character traits and arc, etc. After reading each scene, pause and put up the stickies. Those flashes of inspiration you had while the manuscript was marinating? Put them on the wall, too. If they don't fit perfectly into the scenes, don't worry. If fact, it's a good thing, because if the idea is brilliant, you can reshape the scene to fit it, and that's a good thing.

CHARACTER ARC REVISIONS: LOOKING AT THE HERO'S GROWTH

Having talked about what characters want, let's talk about how characters get what they want. We're going to begin with...secondary characters. Not what you expected, is it? Revision is generally thought of as starting from the beginning of a story and editing the sentences. That's not a real revision. Revision means looking at the story with new eyes, and the easiest way I know of doing that is to look at something other than the main character.

To serve the main character, the secondary characters often mirror the main character in some ways. Remember, though, that we don't want a complete mirror. We want a three-dimensional secondary character like the secondary character who is similar to

the hero but also has marked contrasts. As you think about how the secondary character can mirror the main characters, jot your ideas on a sticky and put it on the wall in the appropriate scene. Like the marinade inspiration ideas, it doesn't matter if the new ideas fit perfectly.

So far, the hero has been driving the story almost exclusively. The goal is the hero's goal. The desire line is the hero's desire line. That necessary focus leads to a kind of storyteller's myopia. We see the story only through the protagonist's lens, and the net effect is a straightforward plot and character arc with few surprises for us or the reader. How to fix it? By developing 23 secondary characters' story arcs. Secondary characters exist to serve the protagonist and/or the antagonist. In doing so, they may serve the plot as well. A well-developed secondary character will also have their own character arc, a desire line that can run in sync with or counter to the desire line of the main character. This secondary character arc can enhance the plot by adding conflict, complications, and tension. This arc is, as you know, what we call the B-Story. If you don't have the B-Story stickied out on the wall, now is a good time to work on it.

EXERCISE TO CLARIFY KEY SCENES

Many excellent novels don't use conventional structure, and there are even more that use conventional structure in nonconventional, inventive ways. When I talk about structure, I am not giving you rules that you must follow, just alerting you to conventions that exist.

When you're revising a novel, it helps to review the Key Scenes so that you remember what you are writing toward. Think of them as rest stops on a long journey. You know all the Key Scenes, but let's double-check them against your current draft.

Most of the Key Scenes are about the hero and not about the action of the story. Also remember that these are Key Scenes. They are not the only scenes you need to tell a complete, robust story, but they need to be polished until they're almost perfect. There are techniques for revising Key Scenes to make them the best that they can be. Try this exercise:

- Make four columns. Write each Key Scene at the top of the first column, the hero's name in 2, the antagonist in 3, and the secondary character in 4.
- For each Key Scene, imagine that you have gone back one hour in time before the scene occurs.
- Under columns 2, 3, and 4, write how each character perceives the hero's mental state in each Key Scene. In other words, describe the hero's self-image, how the Antagonist sees the hero, and how the secondary character sees the hero.
- This exercise will help show how what seems to be an external event is the culmination of the hero's inner struggles, and you will be able to put what you discover on the Sticky Note Wall. Always look for ways to mesh stakes, conflicts, and goals in the story. Double down on connections. Make them mean more.

WHAT IF? THE FINAL QUESTION TO ASK YOURSELF

Look at your Sticky Note Wall. Every scene is on it. Every character is fleshed out. The Turn is now so obvious, you wonder how you ever didn't see it. The wall looks complete, and you're pretty satisfied with the work you've done. Now it's time for the last exercise you'll do with the Sticky Note Wall.

During the drafting process, we reach a point of mental exhaustion. The story is a confusing morass, and we feel like a dog chasing its tail. We want to chuck the manuscript out the window and start fresh (some authors do exactly this, but I don't recommend it). There's an easier way to get back the joy of writing when you and the story have lost that lovin' feeling: ask yourself what if? When I was revising Soul Enchilada, the ending was giving me fits. I was trying to do something structurally specific, but the structure was disrupting the character arc.

Finally, an idea occurred to me: what if I broke my main character's arm? Since the final scene was a basketball game with her soul on the line, having a broken arm would be a very bad thing. I wrote the scene over with her arm broken, and while it added a lot of complications, it made it impossible for her to win, and the idea had to be scrapped. However, in the process of rewriting the scene, I learned how my character would respond to trauma, and I switched the broken arm to something mentally crippling but not physically crippling. The process of asking what if freed my mind off the dead-end track it was on and allowed for possibilities.

That's what I want you to do as the last exercise in this revision pass: ask yourself what if? Ponder the question. Put more stickies on the wall. Keep going until you find a handful of moments where doing a what-if to your hero amps up conflict or stakes to an unbearable level. You aren't changing the story: you are making it matter more to both the hero and the reader.

Write that into the scene.

Once you've finished the what-if character pass and can't think of a single mean thing to do the character, it's time to do one final revision in which you incorporate all of the inspirations and ideas into the draft. Now's the time when you polish the language, fuss over metaphors, and incorporate everything good from the Sticky Note Wall. This time do not take down the Sticky Note Wall. Leave it up until you are absolutely sure that you don't need it anymore.

Poof! You're done! (don't I wish it were that easy)

The manuscript is ready to leave your hands. It's time to turn the manuscript over to beta readers. May God have mercy on your soul.

Just kidding.

Sort of.

ACTIVITIES
DIGGING DEEPER

The contrasts between the hero and supporting secondary characters are a form of tertiary characterization, a kind of cognitive manipulation of negative space that demonstrates the difference between the main character and other characters without ever mentioning it. It may sound difficult, but there are techniques you can use to pull it off without major revision.

EXERCISE 1 (IN THREE PARTS)

Part 1: Make two columns on a sheet of paper. Write the hero's name at the top of one column and the name of a secondary character on the other.

- List four ways the hero and the secondary character are similar.
- List of four ways the hero and the secondary character are markedly different.
- Strike the first way on both lists (the first thing we think of is the most obvious thing. (Try to discard the obvious).

Part 2: In a few sentences, write a short summary of the first time the two characters from Exercise 1 met. What drew them together? Or what made them repel each other? What was the first thing the hero noticed about the secondary character?

Next, write a short scene (with setting, action, and dialogue) about the worst fight the hero and the secondary character ever had. Concentrate on the underlying cause of the fight and how each of them behaved during the fight and in the aftermath.

Then, write a short scene (with setting, action, and dialogue) in which the secondary character gives to /aids with the hero something they don't have. It can be an object, an emotion, a physical trait, a belief.

Finally, write a short scene (with setting, action, and dialogue) in which the hero no longer has access to the thing that the secondary character gave them. How do they react to the loss? What do they realize about themselves? About the secondary character? Put all of the above into the manuscript.

Part 3: Do all of the exercises from Exercise 2 for another secondary character. Put all of the scenes into the manuscript.

STICKY NOTE CHECKLIST: CHARACTERS, DIALOGUE, AND STYLE

- Revision begins with letting a novel "rest" between drafts. It's crucial to step away from the draft for a while. It frees your mind of the story, and when you come back to the manuscript, it will be as an editor, not as a creator.
- Whole novel revision is not starting from the Chapter and polishing the sentences. Polishing sentences is the last step in revision, not the first.
- Secondary characters are often overlooked in early drafts. Revising their B-stories makes you look at the novel with new eyes.

- If you get stuck revising, concentrate on the Key Scenes again. Use the "Exercise to Clarify Key Scenes" to create a summary of the plot like the one in this chapter.
- Even if a scene isn't a Key Scene, it still has to pull its weight by doing multiple things. Check every scene against the SSOD. Are there a couple of weak scenes that can be combined into one scene? Can a weak scene be revised to include more B-Story?

CHAPTER 11
RESPONDING TO READERS

BY FINISHING A NOVEL, you have done what 98 percent of the universe hasn't been able to do. It's quite an accomplishment. You should take a moment to congratulate yourself.

Congratulations!

The moment has now passed. Sigh.

As good as your draft is, you have no way of knowing what is exactly in it. The story that you dreamt is not the story that exists. Now we begin the process of reconciling the version that you imagined with the version that you actually wrote. Luckily, there are people in the world who would be glad to help with that reconciliation.

We call them beta readers.

Beta readers are wonderful creatures. They love to read. They love to read new stuff. They are educated, well-read, and experts in their favorite genres. They have read other books besides yours, so they know where your novel fits in the canon. Some of these beta readers will be writers themselves. Some of them will be folks who thankfully have no ambition to write. All of them will need guidance to supply helpful feedback. It is up to you to guide their reading, and that's what this chapter is about. The best way I know to do that is to use the language of the Sticky Note process. Share with them the ideas of Key Scenes, scene questions, character arcs, and other elements of the SSOD. Tell them what you were trying to accomplish with the Sticky Note Plot process and ask them if you've succeeded.

BETA READERS AND RESPONDING TO FEEDBACK

With that in mind, here are some questions that you can ask beta readers to help you understand and revise your novel:

Why: Ask them to keep asking the question, why? Why does the hero do this? Why does the secondary character react that way? What is the hero's motivation for this? What emotion does it evoke in other characters? Sometimes, it's hard to see these things for ourselves, so we need a trusted reader to help out. When I ask a beta reader for help, I'm looking for specific information. To help focus their reading on the elements of the Sticky Note Plot process, I have a few suggestions for things they can look for.

Story: Did the novel hold their interest from the very beginning? Does the plot make sense? Were there any parts that confused them? Or even frustrated or annoyed them? Are there any parts that make them scratch their head and say huh? Are there parts where they don't believe what happens or don't care so they say, so what? Do they see any events or actions that stretch credibility so much that they think, oh yeah or no way? If so, have them mark those places in the manuscript. These places are where you probably didn't establish the scene goals clearly, or where the characters deviate from the desire lines without explaining why.

Characters: Do the hero and the secondary characters feel like real people? Can the reader remember their names? Do they know what the character looks like? Not just the hero's hair or the color of the secondary character's eyes, but the way they move, the way they dress. Can the reader tell what the hero wants? Does the narrative voice sound like it should? Did the dialogue keep their interest and sound natural to them? If not, whose dialogue sounded artificial, not like a person would speak?

Were the secondary characters believable? Are there any characters that could be made more interesting or more memorable? Any characters that could be cut out? Did they get confused about who's who among the characters? Were there too many characters to keep track of? Too few? (remember the exercise we did to distill our characters to the bare minimum).

Are any of the names of characters too similar? This sounds sort of like bean-counting, but memorable characters tend to be active, and forgettable ones tend to be passive. They are a clue to how dynamic your Sticky Note Plot is.

Setting: Did the readers feel oriented at the beginning of the novel? Can they tell where and when the novel is taking place? Did the setting interest them and did the descriptions seem vivid and real to them? Did the genre interest them, even if they don't normally read in it? Did they feel there was too much description, worldbuilding, or exposition? Not enough? If so, you might have skipped the setting in the SSOD or even when we did the very first sticky wall

Pace: Was there a point at which they felt the story lagged or the reader became less than excited about finding out what was going to happen next? Where, exactly? Did the characters get boring? What parts could be cut out? Did they notice any discrepancies or inconsistencies in time sequences, places, character details, or other details? Were any details repeated or redundant? One trick I use is to ask them to mark where the story slows down for them, or better yet, where they stopped reading and did something else. Many readers stop making marks when they disengage, so make sure they will let you know when they drifted.

Style: Was there enough conflict, tension, and intrigue to keep their interest? Was the writing style acceptable? Did it convey the plot and the hero's desires clearly? Do they think the writing style suits the genre? Was there anything that didn't ring true? Was the ending satisfying? Believable? Were there any unresolved plot lines that they wanted to be wrapped up? If you've used the Sticky Note Plot wall to track them, there probably won't be any unresolved plot lines, unless you're doing that on purpose. Sometimes, though, plots are slippery beasts, and they can get away from us.

POLISHING DIALOGUE: IT'S NOT JUST CHARACTERS TALKING

During first drafts, we put in a ton of placeholder dialogue, thinking "I'll come back to this when I think of something better." And then sometimes, we don't come back to it, and that's where beta readers come in. They will mark dialogue that sounds off, although they may not know why it's off.

After getting readers' feedback is a good time to do a dialogue polishing pass. Here are some things to keep in mind as you do the pass.

WHAT DIALOGUE IS:

- An approximation of human speech that conveys emotion and affects the action of the story.
- Kindled by feeling, made alive by the emotion of the speaker.

WHAT DIALOGUE IS NOT:

- Not real-life: People talk. They talk a lot. Most of the time, it's just noise. Noise doesn't work on the page (except when it's intentional and in small doses). We are mimicking the patterns of speech to shape words for effect, not taking dictation...

- "So I was like, no, not like that, like this. I'm so tired of— he's texting me now, can you believe it? Five minutes ago, he was like yeah, and now, dude. Come on. You going to eat that? Cause carbs, y'know? This cheeseburger's bad eno—ha! Look at this video my girl just sent. Puppies, man—seriously, it's not like that at all. Yeah. Yeah. That's what I'm saying."

- Not a backstory delivery method: We can sneak a little backstory into conversations and into blocking, but heaping helpings of backstory in dialogue is like getting your shoes stepped on:

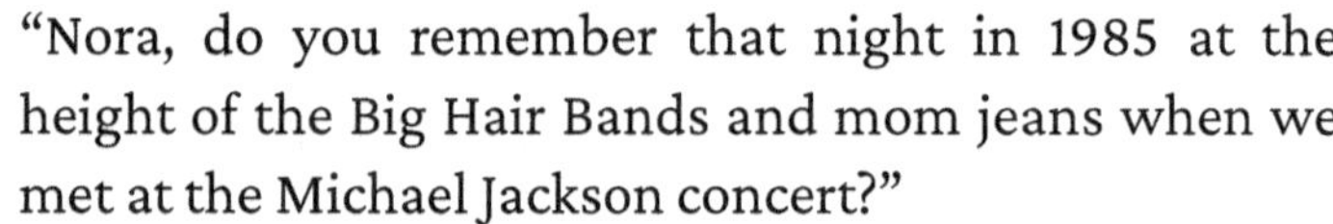

"Nora, do you remember that night in 1985 at the height of the Big Hair Bands and mom jeans when we met at the Michael Jackson concert?"

"The one in Knoxville, at the stadium that holds ninety-five thousand people?"

"Yes, we bumped into each other in the concession line. I was buying a large popcorn and large Pepsi and you—"

"I was buying a large Pepsi, too, and when we collided, popcorn flew everywhere."

"But not a drop of Pepsi was spilled."

"You plucked a single kernel from my hair while 'Thriller' played." "That's when I knew I would spend the rest of my life with you, Bob."

"I want a divorce."

USES FOR DIALOGUE

- *Reveal character:* Dialogue is the fastest, clearest way to reveal character, bar none.
- *Subtext:* There is often dissonance between what a character is saying, thinking, and doing. This dissonance allows you to create subtext, which allows the reader to know things about the character that they may not know themselves.
- *Emotional core:* Every character has an emotional core. They are hiding this core. Dialogue will cause them to reveal it, especially when they are fee ling powerful or vulnerable.
- *Conflict:* Short of physical altercations, dialogue reveals more conflict between characters. It's more nuanced, as well. It's hard to be nuanced while hitting someone.
- *Humor:* Some characters are funny. Some say funny things. Some do funny things. Sometimes, these things are on purpose. Sometimes, they aren't. Dialogue allows humor to flow naturally from a character.
- *Agenda:* Every character in every scene has an agenda. They are trying to complete that agenda, and they do it through dialogue. They want something, and it's usually from the person they are talking to.
- *Lying:* Everybody lies. White lies, tall tales, rationalizations, sins of omission, and big fat whoppers. Characters (almost) never answer a direct question with a direct answer.

That's a ton of stuff for a beta reader to keep in mind as they read, and some may disregard your request for specific feedback, but if you don't ask, you'll never get what you need.

Remember to thank beta readers profusely for the gift of their feedback and be sure to remember them all in the acknowledgments. A signed copy of the published novel would be a nice gesture, too.

What do you do with their feedback? Well, the same thing you do with any feedback. Look for patterns. If one or two readers have problems with the section, it may very well be fine. But if every reader trips over a sentence, scene, or character decision, then something needs to be fixed. Follow the advice from the quotation at the top of this chapter. **Listen to the readers when they say there's a problem but don't feel obligated to take any advice for fixing that problem.** You're the author, and you know your manuscript best.

ENDINGS: HOW TO SATISFY THE READER

Since we are near the end of the book, it seems like a good time to do a revision pass about endings. Everything we write has an ending—poems, essays, stories, letters, and novels. A bad ending can destroy a great novel. A great ending can save a mediocre one. Endings matter for scenes and chapters, as well. How do you envision the novel ending? What will happen to the hero and the secondary character?

In her book *Writing Mysteries for Young People*, Joan Lowry Nixon says that endings should be logical and believable to the reader. She talks specifically about mysteries, but the idea applies to all novels. There needs to be a sense of inevitability in the ending—no coincidences, no *deus ex machina*, no cavalry, and no easy answers. At the same time, books where you can see the ending coming a mile away or worse, where there is little to no resolution to the story, are both infuriating and boring.

Beyond tying up all the major plotlines and having the climax of the story be a memorable scene (it needs to be in scene, not summary), you want to leave beta readers–and all readers– with a lasting image or emotional response to the resolution of the hero's story. What image do you want to last? What emotions do you want to linger? Having left the reader with both of those, end the story. As

Jane Yolen says, **the opening line of a novel is a promise to the reader. The ending is where you deliver on the promise**.

SOME FINAL ADVICE

In her book on being an author, *Taking Joy*, Jane Yolen writes about the best advice she ever received from an editor: "Do not be beguiled by your own facility." In other words, she should not be entranced by the writing skills that come easiest to her. Yolen says that her best skill is writing verse. She has been making poetry since she was a small child, and it is something that she continues to do well.

We all have skills that come to us easily. For me, it is dialogue. As much as I talk about dialogue, I don't pay much attention to it when I'm editing and often don't revise it much, either. You probably have something that you're good at too, and like me, you depend heavily on your gift when you're getting the first draft on paper.

But Yolen warns us against depending too heavily upon our gifts. She encourages us to stretch, to push, and to become skilled in other forms of the writing process that don't come easily.

I encourage you to do the same thing: enjoy your gifts as a writer but concentrate also on the things that you do not do well. Identify your weaknesses and study hard to learn the craft, to overcome these weaknesses, and to make them strengths. Keep working on it until you have many strengths.

I find that inspiration strikes more often and with more gusto when I'm working on a manuscript. If I wait for the Muse to speak, she's off in another room playing with somebody else's manuscript. She needs to be sitting right in my ear for me to hear. Not that I actually believe in Muses. I believe in time spent in the chair, working my way through my manuscripts and making small changes that draw me into the story, which leads me to making changes on the larger story.

Remember also that you really can't begin revising the novel wholesale until you finish the ending and know how it's going to end. Then you go back and begin revising the beginning so that it fits. You have to have the whole story in your head before you can do significant work, but with that story in your head, you're going to find that inspiration strikes so often, you will be compelled to write it all down because there's no way to keep it all in your mind at the same time.

Every novel is different, and we are different writers every time, but sometimes it feels like you're starting over. You aren't. You are getting better. We are all getting better.

Every novel presents its challenges, but there is one thing every experienced novelist knows: you've done this before, and you can do it again.

So grab a pack of stickies and let's plot another novel!

BIBLIOGRAPHY

Barnes, Jennifer L. *"Imaginary Engagement, Real-world Effects: Fiction, Emotion, and Social Cognition."* Review of General Psychology, vol. 22, no. 2, June 2018, pp. 125–134, doi:10.1037/gpr0000124.

Bickham, Jack M. *Scene & Structure: How to Construct Fiction with Scene-By-Scene Flow, Logic and Readability.* Writer's Digest Books, 1993.

Block, Lawrence. *Writing the Novel from Plot to Print.* Writer's Digest Books, 1985. Campbell, Joseph. *The Hero with a Thousand Faces.* Pantheon, 1949.

Collins, Suzanne. *The Hunger Games.* Scholastic, 2008. Cormier, Robert. *The Chocolate War.* Pantheon, 1974.

Eliot, T. S. *The Sacred Wood: Essays on Poetry and Criticism.* Alfred A. Knopf, 1921. Gill, David Macinnis. *Black Hole Sun.* Harper Collins, 2010.

Gill, David Macinnis. *Soul Enchilada.* Harper Collins, 2009. Gill, David Macinnis. *Uncanny.* Harper Collins, 2017.

Hardy, Thomas. *A Pair of Blue Eyes.* Tinsley Brothers, 1873. Hiaasen, Carl. *Hoot.* Alfred A. Knopf, 2002.

Nixon, Joan Lowery. *Writing Mysteries for Young People.* Writer, INC, 1977. Knowles, Jo. *See You at Harry's.* Candlewick Press, 2012.

Lamott, Anne. *Bird By Bird: Some Instructions on Writing and Life.* Anchor, 1995. Lasseter, John. *Toy Story.* Buena Vista Pictures, 1995.

"Parasocial Relationship." Dictionary.Com, 20 Oct. 2021, www.dictionary.com/e/ tech-science/parasocialrelationship.

Rizzolatti G, Arbib MA. 1998. *Language within our grasp.* Trends in Neuroscience. 21:188–94.

Rizzolatti G, Craighero L. 2004. *The mirrorneuron system.* Annual Review of Neuro-science. 27:169–92.

Sachar, Louis. *Holes.* Farrar, Straus and Giroux, 1998.

Swain, Dwight. *Techniques of the Selling Writer.* University of Oklahoma Press, 1965. Turner, Megan Whalen. *The King of Attolia.* Greenwillow Books, 2006.

Turner, Megan Whalen. *The Queen of Attolia.* Greenwillow Books, 2000. Turner, Megan Whalen. *The Thief.* Greenwillow Books, 1996.

Weir, Peter. *Witness.* Paramount Pictures, 1985.

Yolen, Jane. *Take Joy.* Writer's Digest Books, 2006.

ACKNOWLEDGMENTS

et's start with an enormous thank you to the patient and supportive beta readers (IYKYK). Your invaluable feedback, detailed comments, and willingness to deal with typos, non-sequiturs, missing phrases, and dead-end sentences have been nothing short of extraordinary. Y'all pointed out the flaws, cheered the non-flaws, and pushed me to streamline and clarify the steps in the process. I couldn't have done it without your keen insights and thoughtful critiques. You solid mineral material!

A huge shoutout to the folks of the extended VFCA community. Your support over the years has lifted and shaped this process, and it was in the safe confines of Noble Hall that The Sticky Note Plot first saw the light of day. You turn over and over on an axis.

To the many brilliant authors who've used The Sticky Note Plot on their journeys to craft and revise their books, you're the real heroes. Seeing your stories come to life has been beyond rewarding, and this book wouldn't have been written without your successes.

To Katherine Paterson, who showed me (and the Pickwick Plotters) that legendary, award-winning authors can find value in new tools. Your willingness to embrace innovation reminds me that we all keep learning.

And then, Martha Brockenbrough, who singlehandedly turned the manuscript into a finished book. Your drive, humor, technical skill, and sheer badassery made this project a joy to work on. You've been a steadfast ally, a brilliant punster, and a treasured friend. You are a multivariable data table on the spreadsheet of life.

ABOUT THE AUTHOR

David Macinnis Gill is the award-winning author of *Zombie Train, Uncanny, Black Hole Sun, Invisible Sun, Shadow on the Sun, Rising Sun, Uncanny,* and *Soul Enchilada.*

His books have been named an ALA Best Book for Young Adults, a *Kirkus* Best Book, a Bank Street College Best Books of the Year, and an NYPL Stuff for the Teen Age as well as nominated for a variety of state and regional lists and awards. His short stories, essays, and poetry have appeared in several journals, magazines, and anthologies.

He taught in the Writing for Children and Young Adults MFA at Vermont College, where he introduced to Sticky Note Plot method to students and faculty. Over a dozen books have been published using the SNP method, and more are on the way! You can learn more about David's other books at DavidMacinnisGill.com

If you would like a FREE copy of the Spreadsheet of Doom, sign up for the Sticky Note Plotletter at StickyNotePlot.com instagram.com/stickynoteplot

tiktok.com/@stickynoteplot

bookbub.com/authors/david-macinnis-gill

ALSO BY DAVID MACINNIS GILL

Zombie Train

Uncanny

Black Hole Sun

Invisible Sun

Shadow on the Sun

Rising Sun

Soul Enchiludu

Rural Voices

www.ingramcontent.com/pod-product-compliance
Lightning Source LLC
Chambersburg PA
CBHW071745150726
47998CB00005B/1804